W9-BBX-855

Point Addis Rose

Point Addis Rose

COLLECTIBLE
QUILTS

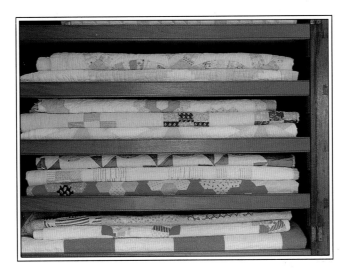

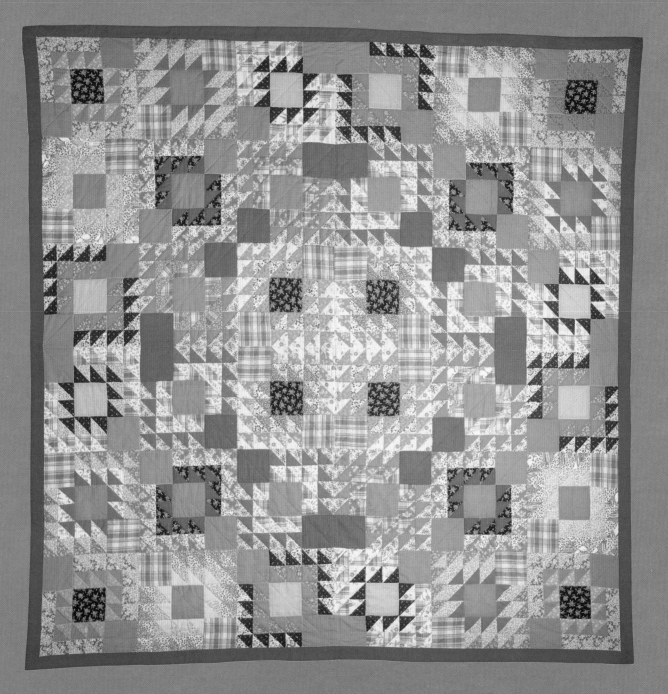

COLLECTIBLE
QUILTS

An Authoritative Guide to
Identifying, Enjoying, and Caring for Quilts

Mary Clare Clark

COURAGE
BOOKS

AN IMPRINT OF RUNNING PRESS
PHILADELPHIA • LONDON

DEDICATION

To Rosie with special thanks

A QUINTET BOOK

Copyright © 1994 Quintet Publishing Limited.
All rights reserved under the Pan American and
International Copyright Conventions. This book may
not be reproduced in whole or in part, in any form or by
any means, electronic or mechanical, including
photocopying, recording, or by any information storage
and retrieval system now known or hereafter invented,
without written permission from the Publisher and
copyright holder.

Canadian Representatives:
General Publishing Co., Ltd.
30 Lesmill Road, Don Mills
Ontario M3B 2T6

9 8 7 6 5 4 3 2 1

Digit on the right indicates the number of this printing

Library of Congress
Cataloging-in-Publication Number
94-72472

ISBN 1-56138-567-0

This book was designed and produced by
Quintet Publishing Limited
6 Blundell Street
London N7 9BH

Creative Director: Richard Dewing
Designer: Ian Hunt
Project Editor: Helen Denholm
Editor: Lydia Darbyshire
Photographer: Paul Forrester

Typeset in Great Britain by
Central Southern Typesetters, Eastbourne
Manufactured in Singapore by Colour Trend
Printed in China by Leefung-Asco Printers Limited

Published by Courage Books
an imprint of Running Press Book Publishers
125 South Twenty-second Street
Philadelphia, Pennsylvania 19103-4399

CONTENTS

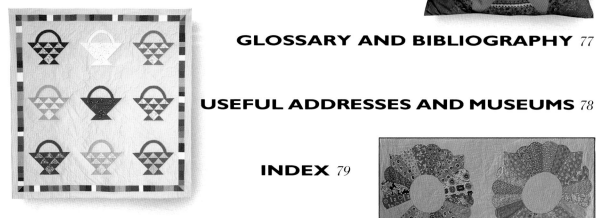
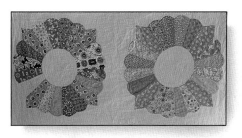

INTRODUCTION

The origins of quilting, patchwork, and appliqué are not absolutely certain, but in the British Museum, London, there is a carved figure of an Egyptian pharaoh from the First Dynasty (c.3400B.C.) wearing what is believed to be a quilted garment. The Stein Collection in the Department of Oriental Antiquities of the British Museum contains an altar frontal dating from c.900B.C. that is made of red silks, in plain and brocade weaves, which have been patchwork-pieced together. Grave finds from southern Siberia dating from c.500B.C. have included wall hangings and saddle trappings that have appliquéd designs of felted wool with a cord sewn around the raw edges of the shapes.

The basic principle of quilting remains the same today – that is, it is a layer of padding between two layers of fabric, with stitching used to hold everything together. The techniques of patchwork and appliqué have changed much more than those of quilting, partly because of the needs of the makers and users, partly because of the availability of different materials, and partly because of the demands of fashion and improving living standards. Most of our knowledge of textiles comes from written or illustrated evidence because few fabrics have survived intact through the ages. Records, such as inventories and supply lists, which include materials acquired and the uses of quilted garments, were kept by the Romans and, in the 11th century, by William the Conqueror and the Crusaders, who used quilting as a form of armor until it became useless against musket and cannon shot.

As the earliest need was to provide warmth and protection for the body, most early quilting was used for garments, and the fashion for quilted waistcoats and petticoats flourished right into the 18th century, although these articles became less fashionable in the towns during the 19th century. In rural areas in the United States, England, Wales, and France, however, petticoats and outer garments were still quilted until

ABOVE LEFT **This unfinished, 19th-century piece in silks and satins is an example of a Tumbling Block pattern.**

the beginning of the 20th century. The quilted silk dressing gown, which became fashionable in the late 19th century, is still popular today.

The use of quilting in furnishings began in Europe in the 11th and 12th centuries, when beds and bed-hangings were introduced by the returning Crusaders. Those who had traveled in the Middle East brought back many new ideas and fashions, including the idea of hanging tents from the ceiling to form draft-excluding curtains around the bed. These curtains were decorated with embroidery and appliqué work, inspired by the designs the Crusaders had seen in the East. Quilted and tufted mats and covers were placed on the bed boards to provide padding and warmth.

The decoration of curtains and covers developed into a fine art in the 17th and 18th centuries, when the bedroom became one of the most important rooms of the house, with the bed being the focal point of that room. Often the bedroom was the only room in which a fire was kept lit all day, and soft furnishings, such as cushions, carpets and daybeds, were provided for visitors to sit on.

This changed again in the 18th and 19th centuries, when upholstered furniture made drawing rooms and parlors more comfortable. Curtains became more affordable and very fashionable, and were used for windows as well as around beds. The Victorians went still further, and visitors were no longer permitted to invade the privacy of the bedroom. At this time lap quilts and covers for items of furniture, such as pianos

and tables, were in common use. These covers were generally not quilted, but were usually lined coverlets. In rural areas of Europe, especially Wales, the north of England, and Provence in France, the tradition of using strong, wholecloth quilting made from wool, linen, and cotton to make petticoats, waistcoats, and bedspreads survived until the 20th century.

Changes occurring in the 20th century came partly from fashion, but the greatest impact was caused by World War I. When women had to work in industry and on the land, they did not have time for household niceties, only necessities, and the popularity of quilting declined somewhat. There was a revival of quilting in the 1920s, when satin fabric was used for dressing gowns and quilts. Patchwork and appliqué were less popular at this time, but they enjoyed a revival in the late 1920s and 1930s, especially during the Depression. World War II had a similar effect on the household as the First World War, and thereafter women never really went back to the sewing of quilts in the same way as before.

There were some areas in the 1950s where patchwork and quilting were still encouraged and taught, but these were few and far between. Fortunately, the Quilt Exhibition, which was held in New York in 1971, and the Great Quilt Contest Traveling Exhibition, which was sponsored by the U.S. Historical Society in 1975, revitalized the art of quilt-making, and today the craft is alive and well, and is practiced all over the world.

LEFT **A representational block patchwork, called Mayflower or Tall Ships, made in the 1930s in Dayton, Ohio, using silk-screen-printed scraps for the boats on a plain ground.**

DATING
QUILTS

Most of the quilts that are available for collecting were made in the 19th and 20th centuries, although there is always a chance of finding an earlier treasure for sale or maybe even in your own attic. However, unless there is a direct connection to the maker, the dating of quilts is not a precise science – it is more like a mixture of detective work and educated guessing.

The most important clues to the age of a quilt are the stitches, the fabric, and the designs used in its making. It must be remembered, however, that fabrics, especially those used for patchwork and appliqué, often started their lives as other things, such as dresses and curtains, before becoming scraps and then part of a quilt, so they may be older than the quilt in which they have been used.

STITCHES

Stitching in quilting will help not so much in dating as in locating the origin of the quilt or the maker. Running stitches were used in northern Europe, in Provence in the south of France, and in Britain for wholecloth quilting. In southern Europe, backstitch and chain stitch were more common. Running stitch was used in the United States for most quilting and patchwork piecing until the mid-19th century, when patchwork over papers became popular. This patchwork technique, which originated in Britain, used an overstitch for the seams, especially if the pieces were not to be quilted.

ABOVE LEFT **This is a sample of European chainstitched quilting.**

ABOVE **A sample of twisted-chain plain quilting.**

In appliqué, the technique of working buttonhole stitch and/or couched cording over the raw edges was known as Persian embroidery, a method used mainly in France, Italy, and Spain, and still known by the French name of *broderie perse*. In northern Europe, Britain, Germany, and Holland, appliqué was usually made with turned-under edges, held in place with a slipstitch. In the Victorian era, decorative embroidery stitches were used over the raw edges of heavier fabrics, such as velvet and brocade, for crazy patchwork quilts.

The domestic sewing machine was invented in 1846, and was in common use by 1865 in America and parts of Europe. The zigzag sewing machine went on the market in the 1950s and was widely used by the 1960s. Industrial quilting machines were in use as early as the 1900s. Machine-stitched quilts were not, therefore, made before the mid-19th century.

FABRICS

The main fabrics used for wholecloth quilts are linen, cotton, and wool. Plain woven fabrics cannot easily be dated, but printed cottons, linsey-woolsey (linen-wool mix), and fustian (cotton-linen mix) can, however, be helpful in dating a quilt.

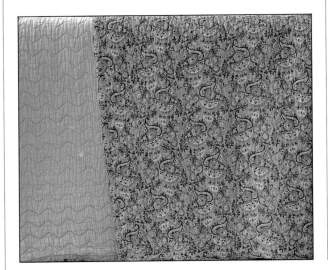

ABOVE **A wholecloth quilt, made with plain fabric on one side and printed fabric on the other, which has been machine stitched in wavy lines. The wadding is cotton. This late 19th-century quilt is of the kind that became a forerunner of the eiderdown quilt popular in the late 19th and early 20th centuries.**

RIGHT **A late 19th-century allover pattern quilt made of rectangular pieces of fabric from a printer's sample book.**

COTTON Cotton cloth, which was called calico, came originally from Calcutta in India, and was imported to Europe by sea from about 1600 by the East India Company. The lengths of cloth, which were block-printed and/or handpainted, were known as chintz, which in Hindi means spotted or printed cloth. Although today we think of chintz as a plain or printed cotton fabric that is glazed, not all early chintzes were glazed. In France these fabrics were known as *indiennes* cloth, and in Portugal they were called *pintados*.

Lengths of these cotton fabrics were sewn together to make a large square, which was used as a bedspread. This was then block-printed and handpainted in colorfast dyes, usually with the Tree of Life and flower designs in the center surrounded by borders. These spreads were known as palampores, which is the Hindi and Persian word for bedcover. The original palampores were printed on a dark red ground, in the style of Persian carpets. They were not popular with Europeans and Americans, however, and in 1643 the East India Company persuaded the makers to print the designs on a plain bleached or unbleached background. After this, palampores became an enormous success – they were so popular, in fact, that by the 1660s the records of the East India Company show the Company was importing 14,000 palampores on each ship. French and English weavers protested at this threat to their livelihood, and laws were passed to stop all imports of *indiennes* cloth to protect the indigenous wool and linen industries. The south of France was not affected by these laws, because at this time it came under the jurisdiction of the Papacy, which is why we have the lovely, uniquely Provençal fabrics today.

Muslin is a finer, woven, bleached cotton fabric from southern India. It was imported from about 1774, and was mostly used for women's and children's clothing; because of its fineness it was not suitable for quilts. Muslin with an allover printed or embroidered pattern of flowers was known as sprig muslin. In the United States today, the word muslin usually means a plain cotton fabric, which may be bleached or unbleached. In Britain this same fabric is known as calico, a word that in America means a cotton cloth with a pattern printed on only one side of the fabric. Because of this double meaning, and to avoid confusion, I shall not use either word – calico or muslin – to describe the fabrics used to make the quilts.

The early settlers in America grew cotton as a crop in the southern states at around the same time as the India cotton cloth was being imported, but they were not allowed to weave it. The only weaving that was allowed in the Colonies was for personal and household use. By law, all cotton had to be shipped to Britain to be spun and woven, so that it could be reimported to America as cloth that was then subject to tax.

LINSEY-WOOLSEY Linsey-woolsey was a linen and wool fabric in which the warp was made of linen while the weft was made of wool that was not good enough to be spun into a long, strong thread suitable for a warp. It is said to have been first woven in Linsey in Suffolk, England, about the middle of the 17th century. This fabric was also woven by the pilgrims in New England, because for many years linen and wool were the only fibers that were available to them for cloth. In 1601, a worsted thread was spun in Norwich, England, which made the wool thread stronger and shiny. After this it was possible to polish linsey-woolsey with a stone, or to size the surface with glue or egg white, which gave it body and a shine. This treatment sealed the holes in the weaving, which not only made the cloth warmer but also stopped the wool of the padding in quilted items from poking through the fabric. The padding was made from wool that was not good enough to spin.

Later, glazed, all-wool fabrics were also known as linsey-woolsey in the United States, even though the linen was omitted. It looked similar to the original cloth and was used for the same purposes – curtains, linings, quilted petticoats and bedspreads – so it kept the name.

FUSTIAN Fustian was the name generally applied to a linen and cotton mix, with a warp of linen and a weft of cotton, and mostly woven in a twill weave for thickness and strength. This fabric was used for wholecloth quilts and for crewelwork embroidery, which was popular for bed curtains and spreads. The threads were mixed because, until the invention of two thread-spinning devices known as a mule and a spinning jenny in Britain in 1767 by James Hargreaves, it was not possible to get a strong enough thread of cotton to use as a warp.

Another cloth that was woven with a linen warp and cotton weft was known as Bolton cloth. This fabric, which was made in Bolton, in Lancashire, England, from 1767, had a looped weft of thick cotton, held in place by two thinner weft threads, which were woven flat. The loops were pulled up to create a pattern on the top surface of the cloth.

DESIGNS

By the mid-18th century, French and English weavers were imitating the designs of India cloth with copper-plate printing techniques. The original copperplates were printed outlines, which were then handpainted, as the India cloths were. These early prints were mainly monochromatic (one-color) prints, because of problems caused by non-colorfast dyes.

The original copperplates were 3 feet square. Some designs, depicting the alphabet, maps, historical events and heroes of the day, were printed on handkerchiefs, and these handkerchiefs were also sometimes used as the center of medallion-type patchwork quilts. As printing technology became more sophisticated, a form of engraving of pictorial scenes, laurel wreaths, and repeated patterns, as in the French "toiles de Jouey," was widely used.

Even after the Revolutionary War came to an end in 1776, fabric still had to be imported into the United States for some years, although cloth began to be printed here almost immediately. One of the best-known printers of fabric was Hewson of Philadelphia, who was also one of the first people to get a grant for his business from the new U.S. government. The history of these fabrics is well-documented, and the fabrics

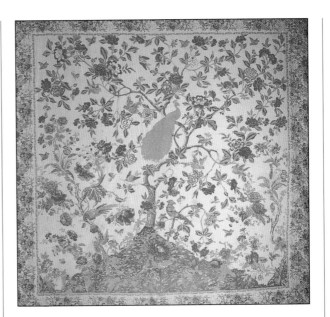

ABOVE **A palampore or Indian bedspread with the Tree of Life design, which has a peacock and a background of flowers all within a wide, flowered border.**

Originally inspired by Persian carpet designs, this pattern was adapted to make it suitable for woodblock printed and painted cotton cloth for bedspreads.

themselves can be seen in several museum collections and books on early American decorative arts.

After 1776 the major East Coast towns began to manufacture as well as to import larger amounts of furniture, fabrics, and designs from France, Spain, and India through the West Indies. This was also the time when pioneers were moving west from the East Coast to settle in the new states of Ohio, Illinois, Indiana, Kentucky, Tennessee, and West Virginia. The settlers took with them the skills of sewing and quilt-making that they had learned in their childhood. The fabrics had to be taken with them or bought from traveling salesmen. Every scrap of material was important, as it had been for the early pilgrims, and nothing was wasted. This was the period in which the block patchwork and appliqué patterns became popular. At first, the fabrics were plain bleached or unbleached cottons, which had to be dyed by the pioneers themselves, or they were woven in checks or striped patterns. Soon, however, printed fabrics began to be available. These were known as calicoes, and they are still called that today, even though they were made and printed in the United States rather than in Calcutta.

ABOVE RIGHT AND LEFT **This copperplate cylinder-printed monochromatic motif was** **produced to celebrate the wedding of Queen Victoria and Prince Albert in 1840.**

In the 19th century the Industrial Revolution brought changes, first to Britain and then to America. The mass-production of cloth led to a reduction in the cost, and it became much more widely available. As a result, townspeople tended not to make, but to have made for them, items such as curtains and bedspreads. People who lived some distance from the larger settlements carried on using their skills and their knowledge of quilting, patchwork, and appliqué until the beginning of the 20th century. At the same time they were developing their own distinctive regional styles, designs, and techniques. Better transport and communication, together with the lower costs of fabrics, meant that rural areas were getting and using new fabrics instead of just scraps. Consequently, the patchwork and appliqué patterns were repeated, and an allover effect was created that was uniquely American.

The designs and colors of fabrics are helpful in dating quilts made between 1790 and 1850, and a summary of the most common characteristics follows. However, this list is not 100 percent reliable because, as we have seen, fabric from scrap bags was often used to make up the tops of patchwork or appliqué quilts.

1790–1800 Dark colors, such as red, brown or black, were used as background colors for printed flowers.

1800–1810 Colors became drabber, with browns, yellows, and olive green being widely used.

1805 There was a fashion for oriental-type prints and patterns on vivid red and yellow backgrounds.

1810–1830 The backgrounds became lighter in shade – often a tea or unbleached, clear color. Dyeing techniques for printed fabrics advanced as artificial dyes became available.

1812 ONWARDS Many commemorative copperplate designs were produced from about this time, and these are easy to date. The ground was unbleached, and the designs were printed in blue, red, and brown.

1815 The copperplate technique became much more refined: it was no longer a single plate, but a cylinder that could repeat very finely etched patterns. The favored background colors were mushroom, green and lilac, and allover patterns were printed in a single color, usually black or brown.

1833 The first solid green dye for printing became available, which meant that for multicolored printing it was no longer necessary to overprint yellow on blue to produce green. Some say that the printing became less accurate, but the development permitted graduated shading and a more realistic or painterly effect to be achieved.

19TH CENTURY Lavender, pink, and lilac were commonly used throughout the 19th century, because they were the colors for half-mourning. Life expectancy was short, especially for infants, and the length of mourning was at least a year.

By the middle of the 19th century the fashion in the towns was for richer, more highly decorated quilts and spreads to be used as lap rugs in sitting rooms. These quilts were made with silks, velvets, and brocades in allover patterns of hexagons, diamonds and stripes, which were used to create Roman Stripes and a Log Cabin pattern, with many variations in shading. Crazy patchwork quilts with very decorative embroidery stitches were also being made in New England during this period.

Hand woodblock printing was still being used for small quantities of cloth. The technique was especially associated with the Arts and Crafts movement in Britain and the Art Nouveau designs in continental Europe at the end of the 19th century. Hand woodblock printing is still used in many parts of the world.

The technique of silk-screen printing was patented in Britain in 1907, but it did not become a popular method of printing until 1926. The technique made it possible to print a freer flow of line and color, and it was not as expensive as block printing or the mass-produced roller prints. The fashions of the 1920s and Art Deco styles of design are easily recognizable in the quilts made at this time.

After World War II, very geometric designs became popular, many with fine black lines and bright, clear colors, which reflected the style of modern paintings of the time. In 1945 the development of the photographic silk-screen printing process meant that it was possible to print from the negative of a photograph and so to reproduce truly realistic designs on fabrics.

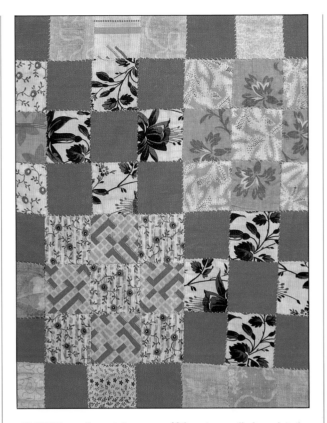

ABOVE **These nine-patch blocks were made from mid-** 19th century, cylinder-printed **fabrics, pieced with plain red.**

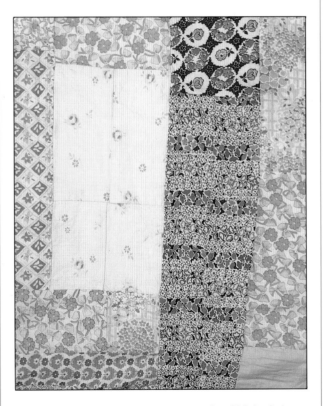

ABOVE **A scrap patchwork sample made up from silk-** screen-printed fabrics dating **from the 1920s.**

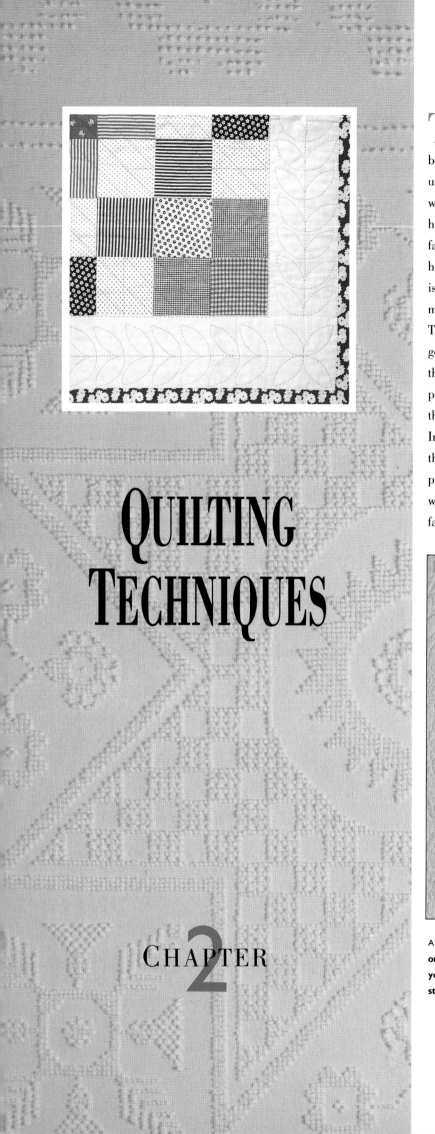

QUILTING TECHNIQUES

The principles underlying the practice of quilting anything were to provide warmth, to protect the body, and to give a longer life to the fabrics. These underlying guidelines have not changed, but the uses to which quilts are put – garments, bedding, and covers – have varied according to the needs and, later, the fashions of the times. The definition of quilting has, however, remained unchanged for thousands of years: it is the placing of a padding between two layers of material, which are then held together with stitches. The three layers are known as the top, which is generally the finest fabric, the padding or wadding in the center, and the back. The most commonly used paddings were cotton, wool and, sometimes, linen, but they varied according to what was available at the time. In the days of the Pilgrim Fathers and the pioneers to the Midwest, the paddings were made of anything that provided good insulation, including the rough bits of wool fleece that were not good enough to spin, scraps of fabrics, unpicked old garments, blankets, old quilts,

ABOVE LEFT **A quilted border on a patchwork quilt on which you can clearly see the even stitching.**

ABOVE **This all-white wholecloth quilt has a central motif of flowers and leaves and a diagonal ground.**

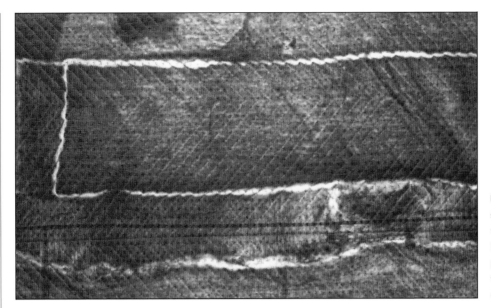

LEFT **This photograph, which shows a quilt with wool wadding illuminated from behind, reveals how the padding was added across the frame as the quilt was being quilted.**

and even corn husks. Paper, which was sometimes made from rags until the 19th century, was also used as padding, its rag content making it an acceptable substitute for more conventional materials.

In the early 17th century, when cotton plants and fabrics were first being imported from India into Europe and America, cotton wadding began to be used in the making of quilts. Cotton was introduced as a crop into the southern states of Virginia, Georgia, and the Carolinas, but the need for warmth was not as great there as in the northern states. It was not, however, until the invention by Eli Whitney (1765–1825) of the cotton gin for removing the seeds from the cotton balls that the cotton was really clean and, as a result, became more popular than wool as a wadding. Wool is still sometimes used as a wadding – in the distinctive quilts of the Welsh, for example, for which woolen fabric is also sometimes used for the tops and backs – but cotton is much more often found as a padding.

Quilts were made on a frame that was the width of the finished quilt. First, the backs were stitched and rolled on the frame; then the combed or carded paddings were laid on the backing in strips the width of the frame; finally, the tops were laid on the other two layers and tacked down, ready to be marked and quilted. The quilting was done from the bottom to the top of the quilt, which was rolled up on the frame as each width was finished. Early American quilting frames were square rather than rectangular, so that several people could work on a quilt at a time. These quilts were quilted from the center out, and the frame became larger as work progressed. Some of these frames were suspended from the ceiling so that they could be raised when they were not in use.

In the United States, the quilting bee as a social meeting of neighbors and friends became as important a part of the pioneers' lives as barn raising and corn husking. When they had finished the pieced and appliquéd tops, the women of the household would call everyone together for a quilting bee that would sometimes last for several days. The large frames would be set up outside in the summer when the days were longer and the light was better for stitching. This was also the time when the announcement of a girl's engagement was usually made, because of the importance of the quilt as part of the dowry and household goods that represented her marriage portion. It is said that each bride had to have 12 quilt tops, plus one special one for her wedding, before she could be married. It was considered to be bad luck to quilt hearts before this announcement, and if there were a vine around the border of the quilt it was considered essential not to break it, as this could indicate a shortened life.

RIGHT **This pink and white wholecloth quilt is decorated with undulating stripes of quilting, known as bellows, feathers and borders.**

BELOW **The wide border of this wholecloth quilt is similar to the borders used for quilted petticoats. The center is covered with a fine diamond filling, and the border is composed of a hammock pattern with leaves coming out of the top and large flowers in the corners.**

WHOLECLOTH QUILTS

FABRICS A wholecloth quilt is one on which the top and back are made of lengths of the same material, whether it is cotton, linen, or wool. More often than not the back is made of a lesser quality fabric, such as homespun, or of leftover fabrics that were once dresses or curtains cut into strips and sewn together.

The most widely used material for early European quilts, at least until the importation of cotton fabrics from India in the 17th century, was linen. Quilting for domestic purposes is recorded from as early as the 12th and 13th centuries, and most of these quilts were made of linen as wholecloth quilts. The patterns on these

quilts were created by the stitches, which made flat and raised areas on the surface.

The early settlers in North America took linen quilts with them, but they also used the linen and wool mix known as linsey-woolsey for quilt-making. This cloth was sometimes polished or glazed to make the fabric stronger and to give it a shine, and this treatment also made it warmer because it sealed the holes in the weaving and stopped the wool padding from escaping through the fabric after quilting. The glazing also made the fabric stiffer, and it was frequently used as a lining for bed curtains and pelmets around the top of beds.

The mix of linen and cotton known as fustian, which was used for bedspreads and hangings in Europe in the

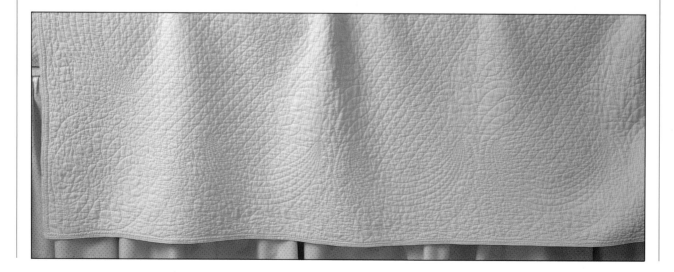

16th century, was softer than linsey-woolsey and used mostly for embroidered crewelwork and, later, for candlewicking covers rather than for wholecloth quilts.

German, Dutch, French, and English immigrants brought their own practices and fashions and a large variety of design motifs from their native countries with them when they settled in North America. Traditional patterns – the heart, cable or twist, feathers and flowers – were used and exchanged with other settlers, until new variations and designs became established. This was also the time when patchwork and appliquéd blocks were being made as tops, which were then quilted. Some of the blocks would be left plain for quilted patterns to be added later. The best known and most intricately quilted work was done by the Pennsylvania Dutch and Amish quilt-makers.

By the beginning of the 19th century, quilting was no longer as fashionable as it had been in the towns and cities of Europe and the East Coast of America, but it was flourishing in the rural areas. Larger-sized pieces of fabric were also becoming available, not only to the gentry and townsfolk but also to the people in the country. The need for warmth and economy were still the most important considerations of the pioneers and farmers in the Midwest of America, as they were in Wales, the north of England and the south of France, and these are the areas where most of the intricately

quilted wholecloth quilts were made until the beginning of the 20th century.

Printed fabrics were being imported at this time, and quilters began to use these fabrics at first for the backs of the wholecloth quilts and, later, for both backs and tops. The use of more than one pattern of print or color of cloth created a wide stripe effect on the backs of some quilts, and soon colors and printed fabrics were being used on both sides of the quilt.

ABOVE **This blue wholecloth quilt, with a flowered tape border, quilted in a pattern of stripes of twisted chain, known as trails, with fans on the outside edges, was made in the** 19th century in the north of England. The quilt, which has a wool wadding, is quilted from one edge to the other, not from the center outwards.

ABOVE **This quilted bonnet with ribbon trimming was made from satin fabric quilted** **with a diamond filling pattern and scalloped edge. It dates from the 19th century.**

ABOVE **Four heart-shapes, in a flower pattern, have been stitched on this silk bonnet** **with satin ribbon bow and silk fringe on the bottom edge, which is scalloped.**

Later in the 19th century, when silk began to be used to make quilts, the fashion for padding changed to eiderdown or feathers to make a warm but lightweight quilt. Very few silk quilts have survived because silk is not strong enough to withstand daily use. Satin is a more durable fabric, and it was used for quilted garments such as dressing gowns and smoking jackets.

Quilting continued to be used into the 20th century, although the mass-production of machine-made quilts and bedspreads led to a decline in its popularity. The fashion for eiderdown spreads began to take over, and the craft of quilt-making stopped altogether with the outbreak of World War I. There was a revival in the

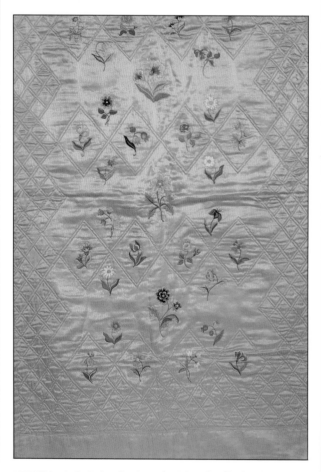

LEFT **This wholecloth quilted cover was made with printed glazed chintz on one side.**

ABOVE **A quilted and embroidered satin bedspread, made between the 1920s and the 1950s, when this type of quilt was very popular. It is in excellent condition because it was never completed.**

LEFT **Quilted in bellow stripes of flowers and a chain twist on a satin weave fabric, this gold wholecloth quilt is decorated with shells, thistles, and tassels on the borders.**

BELOW **A wholecloth quilt, made in the north of England in 1870–80, using a printed fabric with wool wadding.**

quilting of spreads in the late 1920s, when the material used was satin, which was stitched with silk threads and which sometimes had an eiderdown filling. Embroidered designs were sometimes added to the quilt tops at this time.

In Wales and in County Durham in the north of England, the art of quilting was encouraged by the Women's Institute and the Rural Industries Bureau between 1928 and 1939. When World War II broke out all support stopped until 1948, when the South Wales authorities sponsored a survey, the results of which were published in 1954 in the book *Traditional Quilting* by Mrs. FitzRandolph. This sparked a revival of the craft for quilts, dressing gowns, cushions, and other small items, such as tea cozies, and many of these are still being used in homes.

DESIGN The earliest quilts were decorated only with simple geometric designs – squares and diamonds – or shell shapes over the whole of the cloth. Later quilts had a central motif on a background of the simple shapes, which were known as filling patterns, with a border design around the edges. If the center was circular, the filling stitches were usually in squares or diamonds; if the center was a square, the filling was quilted in circular shapes, like shells or overlapping circles, known as Wine Glass or Teacup patterns.

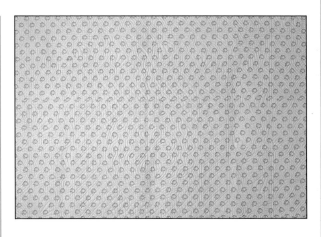

BELOW **One side of this wholecloth quilt is a small allover design; the other side is printed in stripes with larger flowers.**

LEFT **Heavy fabrics with wool wadding were used to make this red and white, 19th-century North Country English quilt. The first red stripe is quilted in a double-diamond pattern with a flower at the center and a wave or fan-shape between. The white stripe has a double row, or mirror image, of S-shapes or scrolls, creating hearts and diamonds where they meet. The third stripe is quilted with overlapping circles that make a flower shape: this is sometimes called a Plate, Teacup, or Wine Glass pattern, depending on the size of the pattern.**

The skill of the quilter was revealed not only in the stitching, but also in the designing of the motifs and borders, especially the corners, to be quilted. Some women were so good at the designing that they were paid to mark a top for others to quilt. The most popular designs were twists, chains, and feathers, which were used both as central motifs and for corners and borders. Regional designs in Britain were made by fishermens' wives, who favored border patterns that looked like

ABOVE **North Country all-cotton wholecloth and strip pieced quilt made with 19th-century copperplate sprig-printed fabric, with plain pink and white strips on the other** side. **It is padded with cotton. The pink strips are quilted with a twisted chain or trail pattern, and the white strips with a bellows pattern with flowers.**

waves and a central motif of a Horn of Plenty or another symbol of safety from the sea. Later, quilting patterns were executed in wide horizontal stripes, not with a central motif with fillings and borders.

Welsh quilts were typically filled in with wide stripes of quilted patterns, known today as Cross Bar, Horizontal, and Double Cross Bar patterns.

In the 18th century, quilting was used for fashionable garments such as petticoats that were meant to be seen, waistcoats and jackets, as well as for bedspreads and curtains. The petticoats were visible under an overskirt of a lightweight fabric, such as silk or cotton, and they were decorated with a wide, heavily quilted border pattern of feathers, flowers, or chain twists, which led up to an open filling, such as diamonds or shells. The more ornate designs were copied from the border designs seen on Indian palampores, which were being imported at this time. These same patterns can also be seen on quilts made for beds during this period. Some of the petticoats have survived, but you are most likely to find less ornate petticoats of the 19th century, which were not intended to be seen. Children's linen caps, women's indoor caps, jackets, and christening robes are more often found because they were handed down through families and, as they were used only occasionally, were less likely to wear out.

CORDED QUILTING

Corded quilting usually involves the use of two layers of fabric, usually linen, stitched together with parallel lines of backstitch or running stitch. A cord is inserted between the two layers and between two rows of stitches to raise the surface of the quilt. Because the cording is inserted after the sewing, holes are made on the wrong side of the work, which creates a right and a wrong side of the quilt or garment. Corded quilting can also be done with one layer of fabric; herringbone stitch is used to hold the cording to the wrong side of the work.

In the 17th and 18th centuries, corded quilting was used mostly for garments such as linen caps, women's jackets, and men's waistcoats, almost all of which were lined. It was often accompanied by pulled- or drawn-thread embroidery, which is called whitework. Flowers, vines, and trees were some of the most popular designs for this type of work. Because this method was padded after stitching, it was lighter to sew than a full-sized wadded quilt, and so was a form of quilting that could be done in the drawing room. The technique, with its fine, intricate patterns, also required greater skill in the needlewoman. Corded

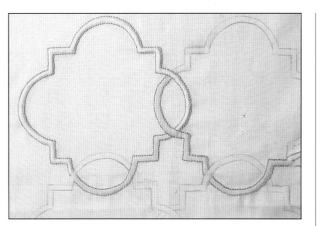

ABOVE **A sample of corded quilting with running stitch on two layers of fabric.**

quilting is sometimes known as Italian work because it is thought to have originated in Sicily, and in the 13th century it was very popular in Italy and Spain, where it was often used for bedspreads. In Britain it was used as an added decoration to padded quilts and petticoats in the 17th century. The style was adopted in other European countries – Germany, Poland, Holland, and Denmark – in the late 17th and 18th centuries, and it is still used there to decorate garments. Corded quilting was taken up in America a little later in the 18th century, and it remained popular until the end of the 19th century.

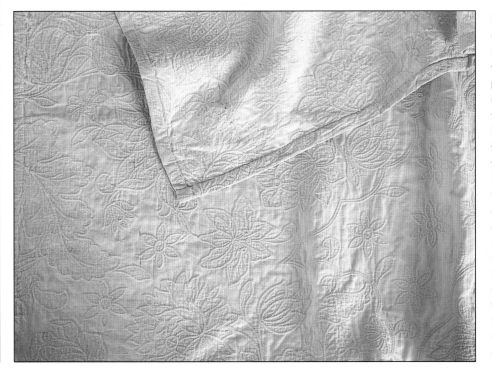

LEFT **The technique of corded quilting, seen here on a bedspread, uses two layers of fabric stitched together with parallel lines to form a pattern, in this case of flowers, which is then padded with cords inserted between the layers from the wrong side of the fabric. This technique, also known as Italian quilting, was very popular for quilts and clothing in the 17th and 18th centuries in Germany. In England, it was used for waistcoats, jackets, caps, bedspreads, and curtains throughout the 18th century. This piece was corded in lengths of plain fabric, which was then cut and hemmed for the bedspread.**

STUFFED AND PADDED QUILTING

Stuffed and padded quilting is called trapunto. It is also sometimes known as bas-relief quilting, for the designs are padded with extra wadding after they have been quilted. This technique originated in Sicily in the 14th century. It did not appear in Britain until the mid-18th century, and it became popular in America shortly after. The outlines of large motifs, such as flowers, are worked with backstitch or small running stitches. Then the background is quilted with a filling pattern, such as diamonds, or an allover pattern of meandering shapes. When the quilting is completed, the large motifs are stuffed with extra padding, which is inserted from the back of the quilt. The backs of these quilts are usually made with a fabric whose threads can be spread apart so that the stuffing can be inserted and then reset afterwards. There is generally a central motif such as a Horn of Plenty, pineapples, sprays of flowers, or baskets of fruit or flowers. During the Revolutionary War and at the Centennial in 1876, the American Eagle was extremely popular.

CANDLEWICKING

Candlewicking is related to the bed rugs and pile embroidery rugs that were made in New England and Pennsylvania in the 17th century. The word "rug" was used for a heavy cover for a bed and not for a floor covering, as we think of rugs today. Turkey-work embroidery was an imitation of woven Turkish carpets, and it was done by knotting tufts of wool onto a piece of fabric to create a pile surface. The technique of candlewicking developed from this technique in the 18th century, and was used to make an all-white pattern on an open-ground cloth. This created much lighter linen and cotton bedspreads, with clusters of flowers, fruit, vines, and other designs used in stuffed and corded quilt-work. Other types of all-over white patterned bedspreads used knotting, couched cords, coral stitches, and French knots. All these techniques created a raised, white pattern on a flat, all-white ground.

BELOW **A close-up of a stuffed quilting pattern with quilted ground.**

WOVEN QUILTS

Marcello quilts, made of cloth woven in patterns that resembled quilted designs, originated in the French town of Marseilles around 1758. The cotton threads appeared to be raised so that the finely woven motifs of flowers, feathers, and fruit stood up against the more thickly woven background. These quilts were made from the mid-18th century to the end of the 19th century. The fabric became known as piqué in the 20th century, and it is still used for clothing and toweling in warm Mediterranean countries.

Bolton cloth, which was made in Bolton, in Lancashire, England, was woven to look as if it were made with knotted or tufted patterns. This was achieved with a heavy cotton weft thread, which was held or pulled up during weaving to create a loop. The raised loops made a pattern that was similar to the quilted and knotted ones. These loops were held in place by two fine threads, woven in a plain weave, which also made a plain-ground cloth. Bolton cloths were made in the second half of the 18th century and in the early part of the 19th century, and were imported into America during this period.

ABOVE **Marcello cloth was made in a type of weave that produces a quilted pattern. This cloth was woven in Marseilles from 1758, and it became very popular in the mid-19th century for bedcovers.**

LEFT **Bolton cloth was made with a weft-pile woven design, here with an eight-pointed star as a central motif. The square corners of the center panel are patterned with leaves and thistles, and the side triangles are patterned with flowers. The piece has plain weave out to the borders of geometric flower shapes.**

APPLIQUÉ QUILTS

CHAPTER 3

Appliqué work is created by placing or applying one fabric to a background fabric, and then sewing it onto the ground cloth with small holding stitches. The fabric on the top can be cut into a shape, such as a flower, leaf, cross, bird, feather, or a heraldic symbol. The technique was used to create the earliest designs that decorated tents, wall hangings, horse trappings, armor, flags, and garments. The earliest appliqués were mostly found in the Middle East, Turkey, Egypt, and in southern Siberia. It was in a Siberian grave dating from about the 5th century B.C. that there were found wall hangings and saddle trappings with appliquéd designs in felt sewn on with a cord couched onto the cut edge, in the technique now known as Persian embroidery.

Appliqué was adopted by European armies during the Crusades. The soldiers used to cover their armor with appliquéd decorations, partly so that it did not shine in the desert sun, and partly to provide some

ABOVE LEFT **A simple example of appliqué with turned edges.**

ABOVE **Made in 1991, this appliqué hanging in the style of a Persian design is worked in the original style of the French *broderie perse*.**

RIGHT **Dating from about 1820, this appliqué bedspread used India printed and painted cottons on a light ground with wide borders. The extra pieces from the border are used at the top corners and in the middle of the central panel. Many pieces of different fabrics form the central motif, but the center is the traditional Tree of Life with birds on it.**

means of distinguishing between friend and foe on the battlefield. The clergy adopted this technique to decorate vestments at the same time, and they both brought this way of decorative sewing back with them on their return to Europe.

This needlework was, therefore, originally done by the men, and it was only later taken up by gentlewomen and nuns. In Britain, the clergy and royalty sometimes embroidered fine canvas with wool and silk threads, and these motifs were then applied to copes, jackets, and other vestments, as well as to box tops and mirror frames, as early as the 13th and 14th centuries. In the 16th century, Mary, Queen of Scots, and Bess of Hardwick, Countess of Shrewsbury, were just two of the famous people whose work has survived to the present.

In different parts of Europe, the techniques adopted varied according to how the appliqué work was to be used as well as to the materials being applied. In France and Italy, appliqué work was mainly for furniture and saddle trappings. The materials employed were leather or stiffened fabric, such as velvet or heavy brocade.

The technique of turning under and stitching pieces of soft fabric, which was used to decorate early Turkish tents, came to be used by north Europeans, including the British, for softer bed curtains and garments. This method, known as basic appliqué, was employed domestically from the time when soft cottons began to be imported into Europe from Egypt and India.

Basic appliqué involves the use of a soft fabric that has been cut out in a shape; an edge of about ¼ inch is turned under, and the shape is sewn to the background with invisible stitches. This method of appliqué was used to sew the motifs to the inside of Turkish tents, some of which were captured by the Polish in the middle of the 17th century when the attempted Turkish invasion of Europe was halted. Two of these tents are on public display – one in Cracow Museum, Poland, and the other in the Historic Museum of Stockholm, Sweden.

LEFT **A close-up of appliquéd flowers at the corner of a Star of Bethlehem quilt (see Chapter 6). The flowers are five overlapping, waterdrop-shaped petals made using scraps of 1920s silk-screen-printed fabrics, with a circle in the center of each flower and a bias piece for the stem.**

BELOW **The basket of flowers was worked in appliqué and pieced with hammocks and leaves on the borders. Fine, plain-colored pieces have been appliquéd on a cotton satin background with cotton wadding. The quilt is heavily quilted with overlapping circles, outline shapes in the hammock and leaves, and stripes and diamonds in the flowers and baskets.**

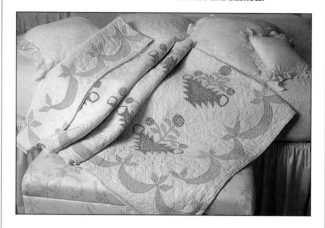

Appliqué using soft cottons did not become popular until the East India Company began to import printed cotton fabrics and palampores in the 17th century. The first imports, which date from around 1606, generally were printed on a dark red ground, and they became more popular when the printing and painting was done on a light or bleached white ground. The first type of printed design consisted of a large square center printed with the Tree of Life on a mound, with flowers and birds in and around the tree. This center panel was surrounded by a narrow, sprig-patterned inner border and a wide, floral outer border. The second type of printed design had the same kind of borders around the edges, but had an allover design of flowers on vines in the center. Both of these designs had a great impact on

quilt-makers of the 17th and 18th centuries. The fabrics were in great demand for bedspreads, wall hangings, curtains and clothing, but they were also still expensive and hard to get.

These palampores were imported into Europe and America at the same time. Because they were highly sought after and also very expensive, they were sometimes used to make not only a bedspread but the curtains as well. This was achieved by cutting out the patterns and applying them to a plain background fabric. The very fine lightweight cotton was more likely to last longer by being supported on a sturdier background fabric.

Appliqué work was most popular in the southern states of America, where the settlers were the first to become prosperous because of the crops they were able to export to Europe, such as tobacco, and those they had by law to export, including cotton. These states were also warmer, and did not need to have heavily quilted bedspreads like the settlers in the northern states and in Canada.

ABOVE **A sample showing a flower made from diamond** shapes and appliquéd with quilted stitching.

ABOVE **This *c.*1920 North Carolina Lily Block patchwork quilt, which has an appliquéd border, uses bias strips for the stems of flowers, the handles of** **the basket, and the wreath around the edge. The flowers are pieced and then appliquéd on the plain ground.**

The early appliquéd spreads were based on the designs of the palampores, with large central designs and several borders. As the fabrics became more freely available in the 18th and 19th centuries, the designs began to change, and baskets, Horns of Plenty, and flower wreaths began to be more popular.

When the copperplate technique of printing textiles was introduced, some of the printing was done especially for appliqué work in the style of *indiennes* cloths. The allover small patterns printed on fabrics are known as calicoes (a name relating to their origin in Calcutta) in the United States, even though they were then being woven and printed there. These fabrics were in more plentiful supply, and the use of different shades of the same color to make up a design of baskets of flowers, or bowls or a cornucopia of fruit allowed the motifs to be more realistic than ever before. Some of these appliqués were done on a small square of background cloth and then sewn together to make up a full-sized spread. The most famous place for this style of work was Baltimore, Maryland, and we still call this type of work a Baltimore Album Quilt. The other name for this kind of quilt is a Friendship Quilt, because some were made by each square being sewn and sometimes signed by friends and neighbors on the announcement of a wedding or a move to another part of the country, especially in the days of the pioneers. Many of these quilts have survived because they were prized possessions, often used only for guests and special occasions. Some of the most popular appliqué designs were flowers, birds, leaves, and fruit. The rose, particularly the Rose of Sharon, was often used for a Wedding Quilt. The American Eagle was another shape that was very popular during the Revolutionary War, and again in the Centennial year of 1876. The pineapple, which was a symbol of hospitality, was used by many early Americans and pioneers in their quilts.

In the late 19th century, basic appliqué work was not as popular as it had been because of the increased interest in patchwork and crazy patchwork, but it enjoyed a revival in the 1920s and 1930s. The large Baltimore Basket was popular as a central motif, with flowers and leaves in vines and wreaths for borders on wholecloth quilted centers on bedcovers. It has become a popular technique for quilters again because it can be used to make representational pictures, whose complicated designs and shapes cannot be achieved with patchwork techniques.

BELOW **The appliqué basket with a wreath of flowers in each corner was a traditional shape for a Baltimore basket** **appliqué in the 18th and 19th centuries. The design was reproduced in 1989 to make a wall hanging.**

LEFT **Appliqué quilt in a traditional Wreath of Roses pattern in squares, with a border of a vine of roses. Shadow-quilting has been used around all the appliqué pieces, with a flower quilted in the center of each square. The border is also quilted with hearts and leaves.**

ABOVE **An example of** *broderie perse* **in which blanket stitch has been used to sew the edges.**

BELOW **Appliqué with a corded edge in the style of traditional French** *broderie perse.*

BRODERIE PERSE

The type of appliqué known as *broderie perse* was named by the French after the Persian embroidery brought to Europe in the 12th and 13th centuries. The fabrics were stiffened with glue and paper on the wrong side, cut out in shapes, stitched on a background, and then a cord was couched around the cut or raw edges. This method was also used with leather shapes for saddle trappings and trunks. *Broderie perse* appliqué was very popular in Italy and Spain as well as in France, and it appeared on garments, pelmets, curtains, and bedspreads. It was later used for soft furnishings, including padded chair seats, cushions and tablecloths, but this was not until the 17th and 18th centuries.

Heavy fabrics, such as velvets and brocades, could be used to add to the richness of the patterns. There were special decorations for royal marriages, including the initials of the bride and groom, and family symbols with intertwined braids and knots to celebrate the joining of the households. These can be seen in many of the paintings, illuminated manuscripts, and tapestries that date from this time.

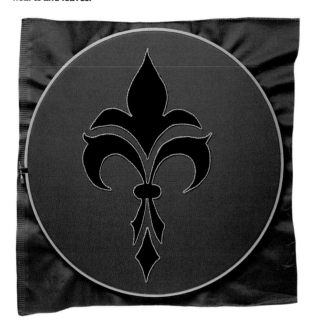

The name *broderie perse* changed its meaning when printed fabrics became available in the 18th century. Since that time the term has come to mean the cutting out of a particular design printed on the fabric. A flower, bird, or any other printed design is cut out, and this shape is sewn on a background with either a turning or a decorative stitch, like a buttonhole stitch or a feather stitch.

ABOVE AND RIGHT **This appliqué quilt was made from William Morris fabric in the 1980s. It was inspired by the original 19th-century drawings for the printed William Morris fabrics. The pattern outlines were drawn for the block cutters to copy, and the center only was colored in to show where the repeat in the pattern occurred. The center has been appliquéd and quilted with the pattern of the fabric, then quilted only. The borders have large, appliquéd Art Nouveau shapes to look like paper holders or a picture frame.**

The use of heavy fabrics and cording remained popular in Europe and America for furnishings, such as pelmets, curtains and tablecloths, throughout the 19th and early 20th centuries, and even up until after World War II. It has become less fashionable since then because of the installation of draftproof windows and central heating; even in very large, old houses the need for long, heavy curtains is not as great as it once was.

The introduction of lighter-weight printed fabrics means that now we can use the same basic appliqué techniques, but can take advantage of the printed shapes to create a basket of flowers, wreath, or vine on a quilt. These are also mostly quilted, and not just plain bedspreads as they were originally.

CRAZY PATCHWORK

The crazy patchwork quilt as we know it today originated in New England in the 19th century, and it was inspired by the patchwork repairs done by the early Pilgrims on their quilts. It soon became very popular throughout America as well as Britain throughout the 19th century.

The Pilgrims and other early settlers in New England did not have much cotton or linen cloth, but they did have woolen material from quite early on. When the quilts that they had brought with them began to show signs of wear and tear, they patched them with what they had. Their religious beliefs discouraged the use of decoration for personal adornment, including trimmings on their garments, such as the lace and embroidery that had been fashionable in Europe when they left for the New World. They were also not encouraged to wear bright colors or to weave patterned designs into their fabrics. Plain dresses and simply shaped garments were the order of the day, and the repairs to old quilts became the only decorative needlework that women were allowed to do. The patches from scraps of old clothing were generally of wool and irregular in shape, and because of this it was not easy to turn under the edges of the fabric, so they were edged in fancy embroidery stitches worked in brightly colored threads that created bold patterns of their own. The quilts were called "crazy" because of the allover random patterns made by these irregular shapes and stitches.

In the 19th century, when new and more elaborate fabrics, such as velvet, brocade and silk, and braids and ribbons became available and were sewn on with silk threads and fancy stitches, the resulting quilts were outstanding. The fashion soon caught on, and in other parts of North America and in Britain crazy patchwork quilts were made by gentlewomen for use in their parlors. They were made as lap rugs to be placed over their knees and also over the furniture. The use of covers on furniture even extended to covering piano and table legs because the curves in them looked like

ABOVE LEFT **A sample of crazy patchwork.**

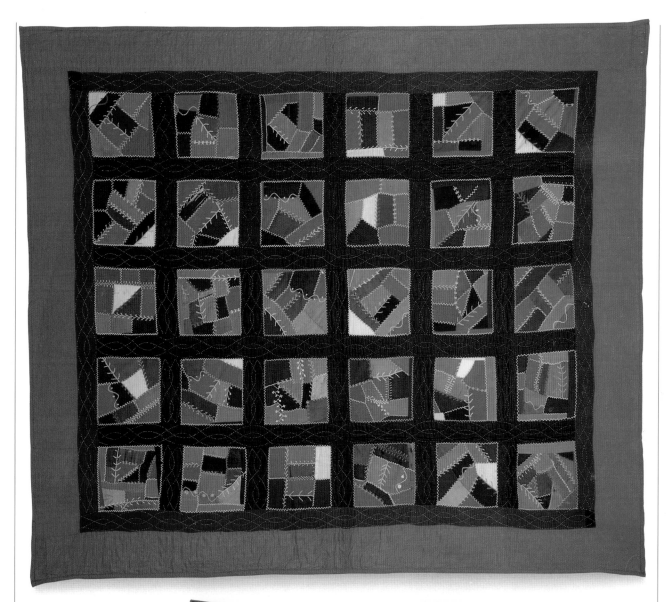

ABOVE **These crazy quilt blocks, dating from c.1890, in a sashing set of black, have been stitched with a wide red outside border. The joins are sewn with a variety of fancy stitches.**

LEFT **This English wool patchwork, with an allover octagon pattern and squares and diamonds in the center, has borders of triangles and diamonds. The quilt, which was made c.1870, is included because the joins of the fabrics are all embroidered with gold silk threads in the crazy quilting technique.**

ABOVE **Two crazy patchwork covers. One is for a book, with a satin lining and the initials of the owner or maker, M.B., and the date, 1880. The inside of the cover is hand-quilted, and the outside edges are corded with** silk braid. The second piece is a handkerchief sachet made of embroidered and pieced silk and velvet fabrics, with a silk cord around the edges and two bows on the top corner. The inside is machine-quilted silk.

ABOVE **Crazy patchwork was used for this heavily embroidered tea cozy, which is dated 1905. It has a gold silk** cord around the edges and forming a braided handle on the top. The inside is silk.

ABOVE **Made in the late 19th century, this crazy patchwork tea cozy of silk and velvet has embroidery and metal sequins on the pieces. It is edged with a** two-color braid that has loops at the corners and on the top for a handle. The inside is an early example of machine quilting.

ABOVE **This large, heavily embroidered crazy patchwork quilt was made between 1887 and 1888 by someone with the initials A.J.T., which appear near the bottom right-hand corner along with the 1888 date. The 1887 date in the center was the year of Queen Victoria's Golden Jubilee, and this is obviously a celebration quilt. The maker embroidered symbols on almost every piece of patchwork.**

women's legs and were not to be seen in prim Victorian homes. Other items, like book covers, handkerchief sachets, and tea cozies, for example, were also produced.

The lap rugs and quilts were relatively heavy in themselves, and were lined rather than having a layer of padding inserted. The patchwork was mostly done on a supporting fabric in a block and then joined with others to make a full-sized quilt or cover. The blocks were often dated and initialed by the makers. Two dates that frequently crop up are the Centennial of the signing of the Declaration of Independence in 1876, and the Jubilee of Queen Victoria in 1887. Other decorations were added to the rich fabrics, including beading, sequins, and small embroideries.

Some full-sized quilts were not so grand as the silk and velvet ones, but were merely woolen patches stitched together with decorative threads. Squares were printed with designs for embroidery to be done on the fabrics in the 1920s and 1930s, and again in the 1950s, but this type of patchwork was never to become as popular as it had been in the late 19th century.

Crazy patchwork and appliqué have moved closer together since the 1950s. Some embroidered and stitched patches are used to create more regular and representational designs on quilts. One by Mara Francis that was in the Great Quilt Contest of 1975, for example, made a whole village from woolen pieces decoratively stitched together.

The combined crafts of embroidery, appliqué, and patchwork are very popular today. Both hand- and machine-work are being used to create beautiful quilts for beds, garments, wall hangings, and other contemporary works of art.

MEDALLION QUILTS

A medallion quilt has a central motif surrounded by a series of borders. The original design layout for this type of quilt came with the first importation into Europe and North America of the India cotton bedspreads known as palampores.

The medallion designs reached the height of their popularity in these areas during the 18th and early 19th centuries. The techniques used in making the quilts were quilting, appliqué and, later, patchwork. The quilting patterns and appliquéd covers of the 17th and 18th centuries were a direct copy of the Indian palampores.

By the mid-18th century, fabrics were still expensive and becoming increasingly difficult to obtain because of the laws against the importation of fabrics from India. The centers of quilts were kept as one large piece of fabric with appliquéd designs using small pieces of Indian calicoes and chintzes.

Lengths of fabric for the borders were harder to find, however, and this is when the piecing together of patches in a strip to make up a length of fabric to be used as a border began to be done. At first these were simple squares, but soon triangles and diamonds were used to make patterns along the border, often with one large square in each corner. It was not long before the corners were being pieced into star-shapes and other geometric forms. It is thought that this was the origin of the block used in later patchwork designs.

In the late 18th century, the copperplate printing process was used in Europe and America to produce some fabric designs that were especially made for the centers of medallion quilts. Early in the 19th century, the center square was turned on its point to form a diamond shape. This was framed by four large triangular pieces, which made the whole thing up to a square shape. At this time, too, the centers themselves were being pieced.

ABOVE LEFT **Cylinder-printed fabrics were used for this medallion quilt with six-pointed stars in a central diamond. The square in the center is formed from four large triangles, and two rows of squares make up the inside borders. The outer borders are of wide, patterned wholecloth.**

RIGHT **The center of this medallion quilt has been divided into four, and the borders are in triangles and squares. It was made in the 19th century from plain red and printed material.**

RIGHT **Early 19th-century copperplate cylinder-printed cottons were used for this medallion quilt. The central motif is an eight-pointed star, with hexagons and half-stars appliquéd around it. Six-petaled flowers are appliquéd in the corners of the center, and the inner border is of pieced triangles with a variable star in the corners. The second border is formed of eight-pointed stars and hexagons, repeated from the center motif. The third border is of large diamond shapes with triangles, with a block of a Crow's Foot pattern at the corners. The outside border is large squares of fabrics alternately pieced with a nine-patch block.**

One of the favorite centers was an eight-pointed star called the Star of Bethlehem. Squares, pieced from the center outwards in light and dark shades of a single color, create a pattern called Sunshine and Shadow.

The medallion-type quilt layout became less popular when allover patterns without borders and block patchwork designs started to be made at the beginning of the 19th century. These were an easier way of producing a quilt top that was either appliquéd or patched in squares and then put together to form a complete top.

The Pennsylvania Amish, of Lancaster and, later, Mifflin Counties, were the exceptions to this move away from the medallion layout. They continued to make quilts like this until well into the 20th century. The Amish of Lancaster County, also known as the Pennsylvania Dutch, used a diamond center with triangles at the corners to make a square, then two borders, a narrow inside border and a wider outside border, with squares at the corners. These quilts were made in brightly colored, plain woven wool or cotton fabrics. When they were double-sided, they were sometimes called Summer and Winter Quilts. Their religion precluded the Amish from wearing printed fabrics, and from decorating their clothes or furnishings with embroidery or buttons. Quilting, however, was permitted, and it was expertly and intricately done with patterns of feathers, chains, twists, and flowers. The fillings were close cross-hatching, in squares and diamond patterns, and these were often worked on the triangles around the center diamond.

This diamond and triangular pattern was called a Cape Quilt after the name of the triangular-shaped, loose garment that, for modesty, was worn over the bodice of the women's dresses. The cape tended to last longer than the rest of the dress, and it could then be used whole or cut up to make the pieces for a Sunshine and Shadow Quilt. This pattern was also very popular with other Amish quilters in the Midwestern states. Although the color red could not be worn, it could be used in quilts, and it was sometimes used for linings and facings inside clothes so that it was not wasted.

As the Amish began to move west to Ohio, Illinois and Indiana, the patterns used for patchwork, fabrics, and quilting designs began to alter. The greatest changes occurred when the allover patterns and block patchwork designs made by the other pioneers began to be passed around the country by visiting families and friends, as well as by the traveling salesmen who supplied the quilt-makers with their fabrics.

RIGHT **This medallion-design quilt, made in 1860, has appliquéd and stuffed flowers in a basket as the central motif, and this is surrounded by two light-colored strip borders of striped and sprig-printed cottons. The outside borders are triangles pieced into squares, which are then joined in strips, with narrow pieces of fabric in between.**

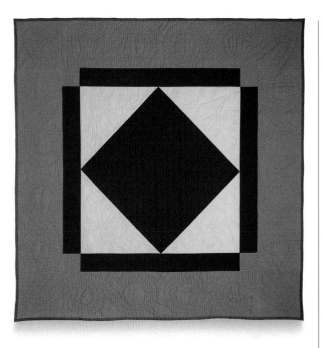

The Amish were making quilts throughout the 19th and 20th centuries. In the 1920s and 1930s, an enormous number of quilts were being made and sold. In country areas, county fairs, at which there was a prize for the best quilt of the year, were still being organized. In Kutztown, Pennsylvania, the fairs were still going strong into the 1970s, with quilt stalls run by the Amish. They made quilts of the highest quality well into the 1970s, but because these were widely marketed and in great demand, the stitching has become less intricate. It is not practical from a financial point of view to spend too much time and energy in hand-quilting. Printed fabrics are bought in for the quilts that are for sale, even though the Amish them-selves still do not wear any printed or patterned fabrics.

The medallion quilt layout has regained some of its popularity since the Great Quilt Contest in 1975, when Jenny Beyer won the Best in Show prize for her outstanding use of the design, and now central designs with borders have become one of the best starting points for a quilter.

ABOVE RIGHT AND LEFT **An Amish-style Sunshine and Shadow center square on the point, with light Cape triangles quilted with two borders, which are also quilted, one with feathers. The quilt was made in 1991. The reverse side of the** quilt (right) has a plain center the same shape and size as the patchwork center. The borders are narrow and wide, with squares at the corners, and are heavily quilted. Double-sided quilts were sometimes called Summer and Winter quilts.

RIGHT **This unusual medallion quilt has hexagons in the center and single rosettes and wave shapes forming wide and narrow borders. The outside** borders are made from seven rows of hexagons in a wave pattern. It was created from copperplate cylinder-printed cottons in the mid-19th century.

PATCHWORK QUILTS – ALLOVER PATTERNS

CHAPTER **6**

There are two main types of patchwork quilt, the allover pattern and the block patchwork design. In this chapter we are going to be looking at the one-patch designs and the two-or-more-patch designs and shapes that create an allover effect on a quilt top.

No one knows for sure when the first patchwork pieces were sewn together. The earliest example I have seen was from a grave find from China (c.900 B.C.), which is in the Stein Collection in the British Museum, London. It is a red silk altar frontal of plain weaves and brocades, which have been cut into squares and rectangles with some triangles on the lower edge to make points. The individual pieces have all been carefully stitched together to make a single, complete cloth.

In the early 18th century, quilts were made in Britain from patches in squares, triangles and diamonds, sewn together in long strips of fabric as borders, to build up a whole piece of cloth that was large enough to make a top for a quilt. These shapes were soon being used on their own for an allover pattern or to make the center and borders of a medallion-type quilt.

The need to piece the cloth at this time resulted from the embargo placed on the importation into Britain and most of France of cloth from India from the turn of the 18th century. Lengths of fabric were hard to obtain and very expensive, so a way was found to make every bit of cloth go further. This was achieved by mixing the plain and the precious patterned fabric together to form the much larger pieces that were required for quilts and bed curtains. Geometric shapes were popular because, if scraps were used, it was easier to get a good design with them than to try to make an appliquéd piece successfully, and the patterns could be repeated for an allover effect.

An excellent early example of this type of patchwork is a complete set of bed furnishings made in about 1708 at Levens Hall, Cumbria, in the north of England. This

ABOVE LEFT **These squares in three colors are sewn edge-to-edge to create a diagonally** **patterned bedspread. The quilt was made in 1989.**

is one of the only surviving full sets of this kind of work, and it contains curtains, pelmets, valances, and a quilted bedspread, all made from patchwork pieced together to form an allover pattern with pieced borders. The main part of the quilt and curtains have a pattern using several geometric shapes, including crosses, octagons, and hexagons.

This type of work, known as English work in America, consists of patchwork pieces that have been folded over and tacked to papers and then sewn together using an overstitch for the seams. Most of the shapes that are in such a quilt are best sewn in this way because of the stretch on the cross, or bias, that is present in all woven fabrics.

Sometimes the papers were left in the quilts to add strength to the fabrics and to provide some additional warmth, and occasionally the tops were never completed or made up into a quilt or cover. Finding the papers in a quilt is one of the best ways of dating it. All kinds of paper were used, including letters, exercise and homework books, diaries and newspapers, all of which would have dates on them.

A good general rule for dating an allover pattern patchwork quilt is by its fabrics. In the late 18th and 19th centuries, cottons were used for most bedspreads.

From about the 1830s until the 1880s, silks, satin, velvets, and ribbons were used, as well as chintzes. These heavier fabrics were very popular in wealthy households, where they were used not only as bedspreads, but also as coverlets and lap rugs for the parlor. Because these covers were not in everyday use, there are still many examples of this type of Victorian patchwork around for today's collector.

SQUARES

The square is one of the most basic and one of the simplest patchwork shapes. Some early pieced squares are quite irregular and random in design because they were mainly made with what was at hand to meet a need, but they do have an innocent charm of their own. These are known as one-patch quilts. At first squares were sewn together from scraps and without much understanding of the ways in which the size, colors and even the seam lines can contribute to the overall effect. These were real scrap patchwork quilts and were not considered "best quilts," with the result that few have survived. They do, however, give a good idea of how greatly quilt designs changed and progressed throughout the 19th and 20th centuries.

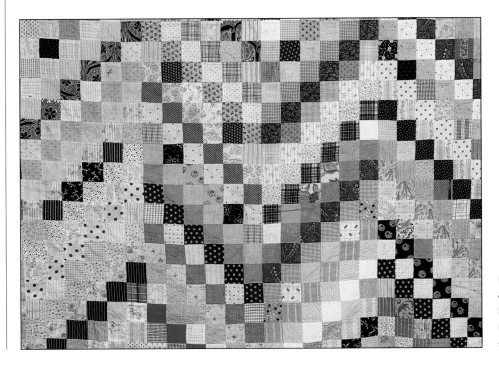

LEFT **Squares of early 20th-century scrap cotton fabric have been sewn together in a herringbone pattern that is six squares wide.**

ABOVE **Large squares on the point, of plain white cotton and glazed India prints known as chintz, dating from 1830–50,** **have been sewn together with sashing and small squares. This is one of a pair of quilts for two single beds.**

The layout of the early examples was generally still based on the medallion-style quilt, but this began to change in the late 18th and early 19th centuries, when quilt-makers were beginning to look at a top as a whole piece and not just as selection of pieces put together in a random way.

SUNSHINE AND SHADOW In the States, squares were being shaded from the center outwards, using light, medium, and dark colors to create an allover effect known as the Sunshine and Shadow design. This was a popular way of arranging simple squares to make an interesting graded pattern.

At the beginning of the 19th century, Amish quilt-makers turned the squares on their points, creating a diamond effect, which gave the pattern a completely new dimension. These quilts were made of plain weave, brightly colored, woolen fabrics. Religion and superstition played a part in the selection of colors and designs. It was believed that if the quilter tried to make a perfect quilt it might offend God, so some quilts have deliberate mistakes in them.

TRIP AROUND THE WORLD A variation of the Sunshine and Shadow pattern is one that, instead of starting with one colored square on its point, has a center made of three or five squares in a line, point to point. Then, when the shades and other colors are added in succession, a rectangular quilt is created.

This pattern is known as Trip Around the World, or Philadelphia Pavement. It was popular in the middle of the 19th century with the Midwestern settlers who were neither Amish nor Mennonites. They used a wide variety of printed cotton fabrics and scraps, and did not put wide borders on them, but carried the patterns out to the edges. The types of fabric used in these quilts allow them to be readily distinguished from the Amish quilts being made at the same time.

All these types of square patchwork quilts were everyday articles produced from about the end of the 18th century. Because scraps were used to make these tops, they are very hard to date accurately, for the fabrics range from the India printed cloths to the cylinder-printed copperplate materials. The best way to make an educated guess at the age of the quilt is to date the latest type of printing technique and the colors used in the pieces of fabric.

These square patterns were rediscovered by quilters in the 1920s and 1930s. As easy one-patch designs for beginners to start patchwork with, as well as a practical way to use up scraps, they have remained popular to this day.

ABOVE **This Sunshine and Shadow pattern has been worked on the square, with** **wide borders and squares at the corners. The quilt was made in 1988.**

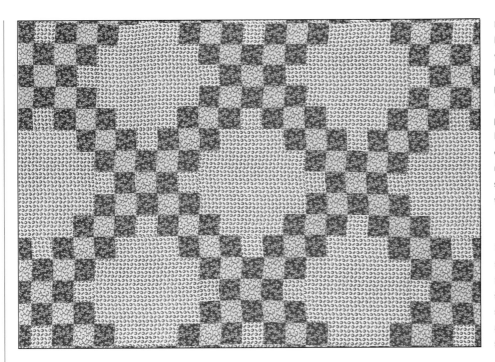

LEFT **The pattern known as Double Irish Chain has been worked in red, pink, and light brown copperplate cylinder-printed fabrics dating from 1830–50. The chain is made of pink and red squares, and the light brown background is of one large square, with four rectangles and four smaller squares sewn to it to make up the steps in the pattern.**

BELOW **This Triple Irish Chain scrap patchwork, worked in the 1920s with five pieces of scrap squares, one row of red squares and blue squares around the plain center, gives a strong diagonal effect.**

IRISH CHAIN The Irish Chain is another variation in the use of patchwork squares to make an allover pattern. The squares can be all the same size, but the design is more often made with a large plain square, usually white, with smaller colored, shaded, and white squares sewn together to create an allover effect like latticework. The large squares are often intricately quilted when they are made up into quilts. The simplicity of the patterns made the Irish Chain popular from the start, and it was practical because the small squares in the design gave the maker an opportunity to use up tiny scraps of fabric.

There are at least three named variations of the Irish Chain patterns – the single, double, and triple. A single chain is mostly all the same color squares and white together, which are turned on the points and crisscross the top of the quilt. The double is a chain of three colored squares, using two colors or shades of the same color and white; the middle square is the lightest color, and is joined on both sides to the next shade or color square. The triple is a chain of five colored squares of three different colors or shades in which the middle square is the lightest, the next ones on both sides are a medium shade, and the outside squares are usually the darkest shade.

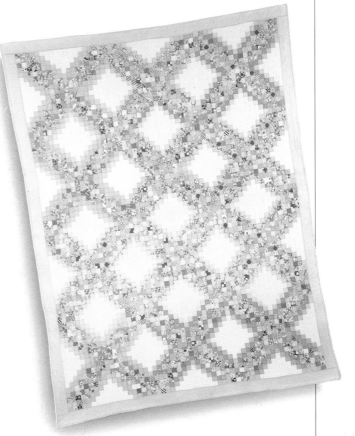

Scrap chains were not shaded, and this gives them a more simple and charming look. Other variations of the Irish Chain are block patchwork made to look like a chain, and these are called the Double-nine Patch and Puss in the Corner blocks.

RECTANGLES

Rectangles were not often used for allover patterns, with the exception of one called Hit and Miss, which can also be made using squares. This design has a strip of patches joined horizontally to another similar strip, but without matching the vertical seam lines, and thus creating a step or brickwork effect.

An example of the use of a rectangular pieced patchwork is a quilt made in the late 19th century, which is in the Worthing Museum, Sussex, in the south of England. In this quilt all the pieces were taken from a printer's sample book, which were kept in their original rectangular shape. It is easy to date a piece such as this accurately.

Rectangular pieces were more often joined to make up strips for borders in early medallion-type quilts, or they were used to form a frame around and between large squares of fabric called sashing. The sashings would sometimes be joined with a small square at the cross point, thereby making a grid or lattice-type of design.

Another use of rectangular pieces was to make the bar or cross-bar patterns used by the Amish settlers. The bars were placed in the center of the quilts and generally had a wide border. Bar quilts were also made in Wales, and these usually had a narrow turned edge instead of wide borders. Both these types of quilt were heavily quilted and made from plain woven woolen cloth. In the Welsh quilts, the quilting patterns sometimes followed the bar stripes. The Amish were using cotton cloth by the beginning of the 20th century, which is a guide to dating early Amish quilts.

A variation of the Amish bar quilt is the use of small rectangular pieces of many different colors, which were sewn together to make the bar. This is called the

RIGHT **This 1992 quilt was inspired by Amish bar quilts. The strip patchwork has a center square and random pieced borders. The wool and corduroy fabrics give depth of color.**

ABOVE **A late 19th-century Amish bar quilt, worked in blue and gold, which has heavy quilting on a diamond pattern.**

BELOW **A 19th-century bar quilt, using plain red cotton with woven check shirt fabrics, which is heavily quilted along the stripes.**

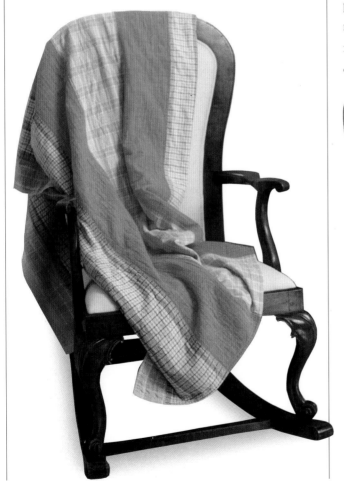

Chinese Coins pattern, and it was a way of using fabric scraps to make up a whole length. The rectangles of fabric were joined along their length in various widths and colors. No repeated color pattern was used when the pieces were sewn together, which gives the bars a pleasant, random effect. The pieced bars were joined to plain, usually dark, bars to make the center of the quilt, and a wide, plain border surrounded the center. These Chinese Coin bar quilts were made mainly by the Midwestern Amish, who did not include printed fabrics, but the use of contrasting colors produced stunning quilts.

LOG CABIN

In this book the Log Cabin, Pineapple, and Courthouse Steps patterns of patchwork are considered as allover patterns and not as block patchworks, even though they are made up of squares in the same way as crazy patchwork. The reason for this is that the patterns do not stand up by themselves, but depend on the way that individual pieces are placed next to the other pieces to create the allover patterns that give rise to their names.

ABOVE **The Log Cabin pattern was popular in the mid-19th century in both America and England for parlor knee rugs** **and furniture covers. This patchwork, in Light and Dark pattern, was made with silk and satin fabrics and ribbons.**

LEFT **An example of Log Cabin.**

The most common arrangements for the Log Cabin pattern are Light and Dark, Straight Furrows, Streak of Lightning, and Barn Raising. Log Cabin was a very popular form of patchwork in the early 19th century in the United States, and it spread to Britain in the middle of the century along with crazy patchwork. The quilts were made on a base of fabric that provided some reinforcement for the fine silks and supported the heavy fabrics, like velvets, that were fashionable at that time. Because of this these quilts have lasted a long time and can still be found for sale.

A typical Log Cabin pattern starts with a small square in the center of a large square of base fabric, which is the finished size of the pattern. The small squares in the center are usually all the same color, traditionally red. The rectangular strips are all the same width but vary in length. They are stitched to each other and to the base, progressing around the center. The shading is done with the light and dark pieces making right angles on opposite sides of the base square.

In Barn Raising, the allover effect is a central diamond shape in the light shades of fabrics, with the

RIGHT **This Log Cabin variation is known as a Light and Dark pattern. The late 19th-century quilt is made in two plain-colored cotton fabrics with a crocheted edge. The plain blocks at the corners and lower edge are pieced in strips of white, to give a white on white effect.**

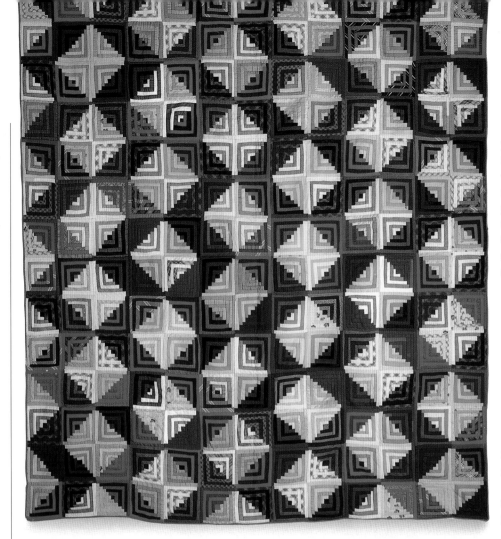

LEFT **An 1880 Log Cabin patchwork in a Streak of Lightning or Zigzag pattern, with a light diamond in the negative space. Plain and printed fabrics have been used throughout. Every other strip in the Log Cabin pattern is the same fabric, which creates a striking effect.**

BELOW **Scraps of silk-screen-printed fabrics, dating from the 1920s and 1930s, were used to make this quilt in a Pineapple pattern on a square grid.**

contrasting pieces of the squares making a frame. The dark pieces of the next row are sewn to the dark sides of the center. The light and dark pieces alternate to create a strong diamond frame that increases in size until the whole top has been made.

The Light and Dark pattern is made by joining four light and four dark patterns to make a checkerboard or diamond effect. Straight Furrows consists of light and dark straight diagonal lines, and its name comes from its resemblance to a ploughed field. Streak of Lightning is a zigzag effect made to resemble a bolt of lightning.

Both Courthouse Steps and Pineapple were made at the same time as the Log Cabin quilts, but neither was quite as popular a design. Courthouse Steps is a variation of Log Cabin, but the light and dark rectangles are directly opposite each other, not at right angles. The Pineapple or Windmill Blades pattern is a more intricate combination of a square in the center with triangles and rectangles sewn together to make a vibrant turning pattern.

STRIP OR STRING PATCHWORK

Sometimes scrap pieces, probably rectangular or string-like to start with, were sewn together to make a larger piece of fabric that was then used as a square in a Roman Stripe pattern or cut into a shape, like a diamond, and pieced as an eight-pointed star. The earliest examples of the star-shapes come from the late 18th century, when the diamonds were cut either along or across the strips, depending on the finished effect the maker wanted to achieve.

TRIANGLES

Like squares, triangles are simple geometric shapes that can make many beautiful and surprising allover patterns. Two main kinds of triangles are used to make patchwork tops. One is a half of a square, or a right-angled triangle; the other is made from a square that has been quartered, and is called an isosceles triangle. Equilateral triangles can also be used, that is to say triangles in which all the sides are the same length.

Each type of triangle makes very different patterns, but these mostly depend on the colors used to highlight the shapes in the patterns. The earliest use of triangles was in borders of medallion-type quilts, when half-squares were used in pairs, with a light- and a dark-colored triangle being used to make up a square. These squares were sewn together in a strip and the effect, named the Sawtooth pattern, was a popular edging around quilts.

Equilateral triangles, which resemble a half-diamond shape, are pieced in alternate colors, light and dark, to give an effect that is more like a stripe than a square, and some of the most effective patterns have been made when every other triangle on the whole top is the same color and the alternate ones are scraps or a much darker shade.

LEFT **A mosaic of tweed triangles in wool cloth, with narrow and wide borders, was used to make this throw-over or knee rug in 1988.**

ABOVE **Triangles in a Flying Geese pattern form a traditional design, with the large triangles in dark colors and the smaller ones in light** **colors. The triangles are sewn with dark wholecloth strips in between. This 1991 quilt is an effective example of a strip patchwork quilt.**

SUGAR LOAF This pattern is made up of two large isosceles triangles. One is a whole piece of plain-colored cloth, the other consists of small diamonds pieced together. The diamonds are in contrasting light and dark shades of a single color, and the pattern gets its name because in the early 19th century sugar, which was often hard to come by, was sold in multicolored, cone-shaped packages. A good pantry would have a store of the sugar cones, and it is thought that this was the inspiration for the quilt-makers.

FLYING GEESE The Flying Geese pattern was made from the late 18th century onwards. It was made from different types of triangles sewn in strips, and these alternated with bars of fabric, the same width but not pieced, which were placed between each strip of triangles. The pattern was named after the geese that migrated twice yearly to and from Canada across most

of America. It is usually made with large, bright, multicolored, quarter-square triangles, with light colors or white used for smaller, half-square triangles. These small triangles are stitched to the sides of the larger one to make a rectangle. A long strip is made by sewing these pieces together with all the large triangles pointing in the same direction. Then the plain strips are added. In the 19th century, fine cylinder-printed fabrics were used for the rows between the flying geese pattern and for the borders. Because the triangles were made from scraps, it is best to date this type of quilt from the rows of whole fabric. This pattern was made in the East Coast states and in the Midwest from the late 18th century and throughout the 19th century.

OCEAN WAVES This allover pattern uses large, plain squares with the triangles. Like the Log Cabin patterns, it could be regarded as a block patchwork, but it is not effective without the other pieces, and therefore it is really an allover pattern type of quilt. The pattern is made with a center square, usually plain white fabric, and rows of half-square triangles sewn to each other in squares turned on the points. This makes a wave-like effect, especially when one of the triangles is the same fabric as the center square.

ABOVE **Cotton was used for these Flying Geese and Arrows patchwork cushions, based on** **traditional Amish designs, to create a modern (1989) graphic effect.**

DIAMONDS

Diamonds were common in British and American patchwork in the late 18th century. These shapes were best worked over papers, and were more treasured than the simple square patterns. The earliest and one of the most popular designs made from diamonds was an eight-pointed star known as the Star of Bethlehem; it was also called the Lone Star, Star of the East, and Rising Star. The colors of the fabrics were arranged in shades, ranging from light to dark, to produce a radiating effect. The star made a brilliant center design that would have incorporated both plain squares and

triangles, which were either heavily quilted or appliquéd with flowers, to make up the large piece used for the center panel of a quilt.

These quilts were harder to make, and they were, therefore, only used for special guests and on important occasions. The name Star of Bethlehem made it a particular favorite for use at Christmastime, when households welcomed in visitors. Because they were regarded as special, many examples have survived in excellent condition. Cotton was the most commonly used fabric for this type of quilt, but later in the 19th century some heavier fabrics began to be used to make this pattern.

LEFT **An eight-pointed star made from diamonds.**

BELOW **A simple example of Tumbling Blocks.**

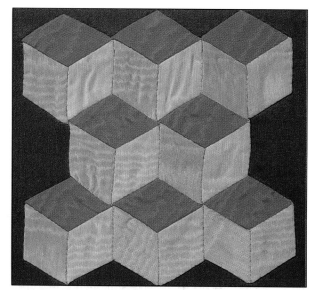

LEFT **Diamonds and triangles with circles have been used to make two four-pointed stars, one pink, the other green, in this variation of a Key West Beauty pattern. Plain fine cotton fabrics were used, and the piece has been heavily quilted in large, overlapping semicircles, known as a Wave pattern.**

ABOVE **This 19th-century diamond-pattern quilt top is of large plain and small patterned silk and satin fabrics stitched over papers. The quilt is unfinished and still has the papers in the back of the pieces, which are oversewn together. If you find a quilt with papers left in, it may be easier to date.**

BELOW **Diamonds of mid-19th-century copperplate cylinder prints were used to make six-pointed stars, with plain white hexagons between them. The quilt is heavily quilted in bands of twisted chain or trail patterns and bellows with flowers.**

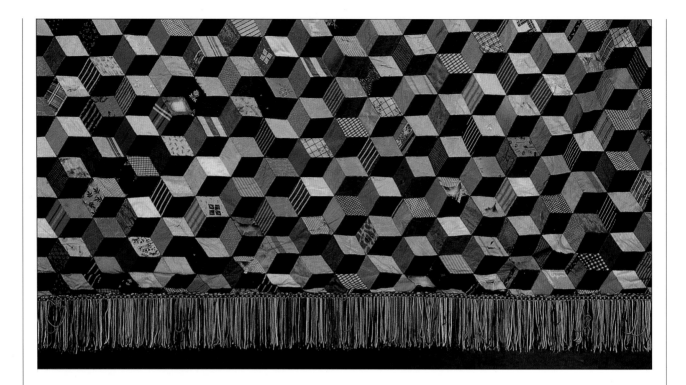

TUMBLING BLOCK Tumbling Block patterns were made with a diamond in an allover pattern from the late 18th century until the middle of the 19th century. Early examples were mostly produced using cotton fabrics, but from the beginning of the 19th century the tops were made of silks and satins. In the 20th century cotton began to be used again, and a larger diamond, called a Baby Block or Building Block pattern, became popular. These quilts were often made in more pastel and subtle colors and shades than the earlier ones.

A Tumbling Block design is composed of three diamond-shaped pieces of patchwork, one in each of the shades of light, medium, and dark. The shades are always sewn to point in the same direction, thus creating the three-dimensional effect of a cube. The pattern was formerly always made over papers, and these were sometimes left in the tops, which is an excellent clue to dating a quilt.

RIGHT **A Tumbling Block design was used for this late 19th-century cushion cover, made of silk and satin fabrics and ribbons, and with a velvet back. The three-dimensional** effect of the blocks is not as marked as in the quilt above because the light, medium and dark shades are not arranged consistently.

ABOVE **The Tumbling Block pattern, formed of hexagons, was made of silk diamonds sewn together to resemble cubes of turning blocks. The effect is created by using dark, medium and light shades,** arranged in the same order, for every hexagon. The cover is not quilted but lined, and it has a long silk fringe on the edge. It is full size, and was made between 1865 and 1875 in Britain.

HEXAGONS

The hexagon or honeycomb patchwork patterns were inspired by mosaic tile designs used by the Romans and in Middle Eastern countries. This is a form of patchwork that has been popular for many centuries, and it is a traditional British technique. The basic shape of a hexagon requires careful planning and skilled cutting out and sewing. For these reasons, the fabric was always sewn onto paper patterns and an oversewing stitch was used to make the seams. This was frequently the first patchwork design taught to British girls in the mid-19th century, and because the shapes were small, the quilt could be stitched in the parlor or drawing room.

Many different allover patterns can be created by the junction of a center hexagon and subsequent rows of the same shape. Diamonds, stars, and sometimes heart-shapes were made at a comparatively early stage, but the most usual pattern made by the hexagons is a rosette, which is a single hexagon, usually in a light color, surrounded by six differently colored hexagons. The joining of one or more rows around this creates a larger rosette. These are then joined together with a background hexagon of a plain fabric, usually of a contrasting color, such as white, green, or black. These patterns are known as the Flower Garden or Grandmother's Flower Garden, and they have developed into an intricate, allover pattern. In the late 19th century, flowers printed on different fabrics were

BELOW **Made between 1820 and 1850, this silk hexagon pieced patchwork was probably made to go over a piece of furniture – like a table for example. The red central hexagon is surrounded by alternate rows of light and dark shades of silk. The last five rows of hexagons turn the light and dark shades away from the center, and create a fringe effect in the pattern.**

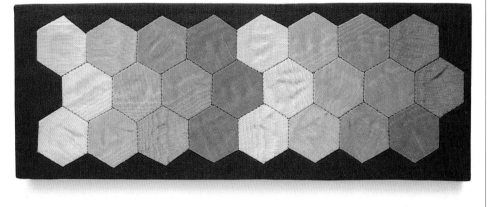

ABOVE **A sample of hexagons in a wave pattern.**

ABOVE **Hexagons of scraps of 19th-century copperplate cylinder-printed fabrics have been used in a single rosette on a white ground, with a cotton fringe.**

BELOW **Hexagons have been arranged in a diamond pattern,** the center of which consists of four hexagons with two rows of hexagons around them to create the diamond shape. The fabrics are glazed chintz, dating from 1860–90, and they are still glazed. The allover effect is of a Middle Eastern carpet or mosaic tiles.

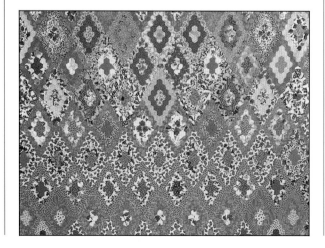

picked out for each hexagon and built up into a wreath of flowers in the center of the quilt. Some hexagon patterns are made up of a combination of colors to create wavy lines that were used along the borders of the garden quilts.

Papers may be found in early quilts, and any that were not finished. Most hexagonal quilts were not padded or quilted, only lined, so leaving in the papers made the shapes stay flat and helped them to last longer. Some of these quilts were made of cotton, which meant that they were not particularly durable, but the silk ones have survived better.

Hexagons are also mixed with other shapes, like triangles and diamonds. When diamonds are joined to make a six-pointed star, the space between the stars is a hexagon. Hexagons with elongated sides, which are known as Church Windows, are a useful shape that can be used with squares in between to create an octagonal, stone-tiled-floor effect.

LEFT **The large hexagons in a double rosette pattern with a single blue ground were worked in glazed chintz fabrics between 1830 and 1850. The plain blue cotton border suggests that this may have once been a larger quilt.**

BELOW **Hexagons were used to create the Grandmother's Flower Garden pattern, with the flowers and butterflies in the fabrics helping to create an allover effect of a wreath and border that is a modern (1992) progression from the 1920s hexagon pattern.**

ABOVE **This 1991 kimono hanging was made entirely from a family kimono belonging to the grandmother** of the maker and worn at her wedding. The small white flowers are the family's symbol.

BELOW **Large silk hexagons in a single rosette on a black ground have been used on this typical 19th-century drawing** room coverlet, which was popular in England and America.

LEFT **This hexagon quilt, with a double rosette of plain yellow centers, with one row of plain green and an outside row of 19th-century printed fabrics, mostly of a golden color, has a** plain white ground. The border is also a double row of pale green hexagons, making a scalloped effect. It is quilted all over with an outline pattern of hexagons.

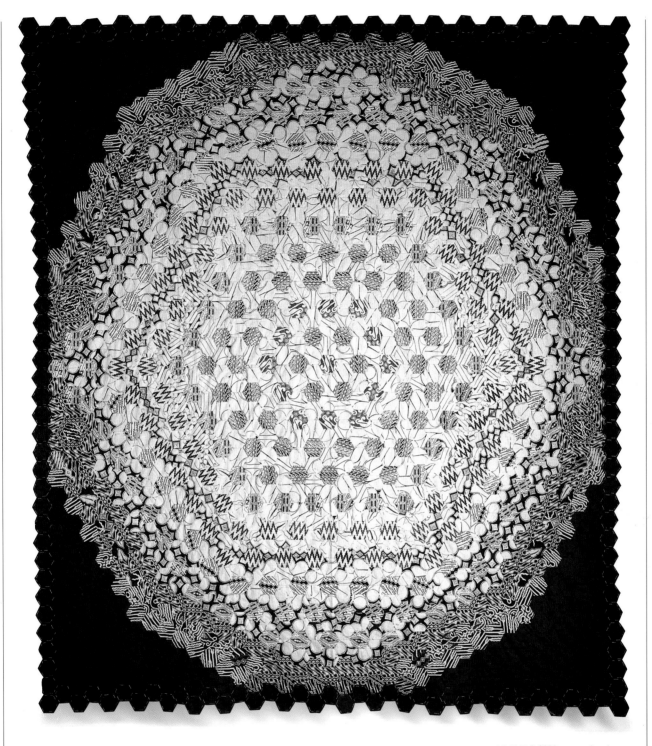

OPPOSITE **Hexagons have been used in a mosaic pattern with an allover star effect. This is a 19th-century tablecloth, which has been heavily embroidered with silk threads and beads. There is silk cording around the edges, and the corners have beautiful Chinese tassels attached to them.**

ABOVE **A 1992 example of an allover pattern scrap quilt uses hexagons of indigo-dyed cottons to create a circular shape, going from light to dark.**

PATCHWORK QUILTS - BLOCKS

We know that patchwork quilts were being made in allover patterns from early in the 18th century in both Britain and the United States. In the United States, block patterns began to be used in patchworks in the late 18th century, although they did not become fashionable until almost the mid-19th century. They reached the height of their popularity at the beginning of the 20th century, when several publications appeared that included patterns and design suggestions for quilts. These included *Godey's Lady's Book*, 1851, *The Ladies' Friend*, 1866, *Ladies' Home Journal*, 1896, *Ladies' Art Company*, 1898, *Practical Needlework*, 1910, *Ladies' Art Journal*, 1928, *Grandmother Clark's Authentic Early American Quilts*, 1932, *Romance of Patchwork Quilts in America*, 1935, *The Standard Book of Quiltmaking and Collecting*, 1949, *The Perfect Patchwork Primer*, 1973, and *The Quilter's Album of Blocks and Borders*, 1980. Fabric companies and distributors, such as Sears & Roebuck, produced kits for the difficult patterns, including Dresden Plate, *c.*1890, and Double Wedding Ring, *c.*1910, and these helped to make block patchwork very popular. All the shapes in the kits were pre-cut and color coordinated, so that the patchworker could make a difficult quilt top with confidence.

The block was a useful way of making up a top for a quilt when the first American settlers started moving to the Midwestern states in the aftermath of the Revolutionary War. Blocks had been made before this time, but they were mainly used as corners on wide borders of medallion-type quilts. Another kind of block that was popular in the late 18th century was the appliquéd square, which was known as the Album Block or Baltimore Block. These were made up into Friendship Quilts, and they sometimes, although rarely, included patchwork blocks. The block quilts discussed in this chapter are all patchwork-pieced blocks.

ABOVE LEFT **A sample of a four-patch block, one of the simplest patchwork blocks.**

ABOVE **An eight-pointed star in the Lily pattern.**

LEFT **A sample of a nine-patch block worked into the Cherry Basket.**

The early settlers, especially those in the new territories of Ohio, Indiana and Illinois, were among the most prolific patchworkers of all time. They made their own patterns from folded paper squares, and these designs were named after the states themselves and after leaves, stars, hearts, birds, flowers, and even after hard times, like Rocky Road to Kansas. In fact, blocks were named after almost anything, including historical and political events – Old Tippecanoe, Lincoln's Platform, Sherman's March, and Tail of Benjamin Franklin's Kite to mention just a few.

The first blocks were made by folding a square of paper, the finished size of the patchwork block, into either four or nine sections. These are still called the four-patch block and the nine-patch block. To get the four-patch design the paper was folded in half, then in half again. If the patchworker wanted triangles in the corners, the paper would be folded again from the center point out to the edges to make triangular shapes across the squares, and this pattern was called Fan Mill or Crow's Foot. For a nine-patch block the papers would be folded into thirds in both directions across the square. These two ways of dividing the squares were the most often used, but there were many more variations. Patterns and designs were exchanged and passed down from mother to daughter, as well as given to neighbors who came for a quilting bee, or to acquaintances who were passing through.

Throughout most of the 19th century the source of fabrics in these states was the traveling salesman, who was another means by which patterns and designs for quilts could be passed on. Country fairs offered opportunities to show off skills and new ideas, and there were prizes for the quilt of the year and the best in show. These fairs continued to be held until the outbreak of World War I, and although they were revived in the 1920s and 1930s, they stopped again during World War II. There was a short-lived revival in the 1950s, but this type of work only really took off again in the 1970s, with the Great Quilt Exhibition. Today, interest in block patchwork and quilting has spread and become popular all over the world.

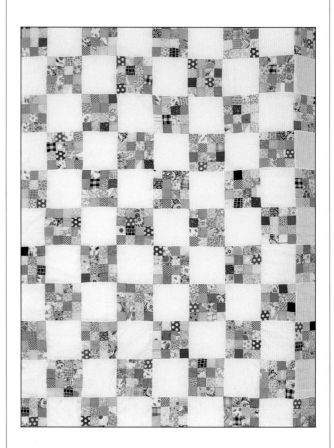

ABOVE **Curved block patchwork in the Drunkard's Path pattern.**

ABOVE **This sixteen-patch block patchwork, in a pieced** and plain set, was made in the **1920s from scraps of fabric.**

LEFT **Known as the Indiana Puzzle or Snail Trail, this four-patch design creates great movement. The quilt illustrated is a modern interpretation, made in 1992, and it uses a variety of different fabrics and colors to create a beach, waves, and sea effect across the quilt.**

The early tops were made of a mix of fabrics, and they were not as carefully planned as later quilts. Most were made from scraps of fabric left over from cutting out dresses and shirts, or from pieces saved from worn-out garments. The scrap-bag was an essential, kept by all quilt-makers and handed down from generation to generation. Some of the fabrics would have spanned as many as 50 years and reflected much family history. As with the allover patterned quilts, the fabrics used in these quilts can give a hint as to what was in the scrap-bag but not an accurate indication of the date the quilt was actually stitched.

Large quantities of quilts and tops were made between 1800 and 1880 in nearly every American family. Every girl was expected to make at least 13 quilts of her own before she was married – 12 were made while she was growing up, and a thirteenth would be quilted on the announcement of her wedding. If a family had three daughters, there might be as many as 36 quilts in that one house before any of the daughters announced her intention of marrying. Moreover, most women went on to make more quilts and tops after their marriage – hardly surprising if they expected to have as many as a dozen children, which was not unusual. They also used these quilt tops to teach the craft to their daughters.

From the middle of the 19th century, as improved means of communication and travel came to the Midwest and western states, and as railroads made the shops in the larger towns more accessible, the quilters could buy a variety of fabrics more easily. American weavers and printers began to produce cotton cloth, which was less expensive than the imported fabrics, so that whole pieces of cloth could be bought to make a quilt instead of just scraps.

The quilts made with new cloth in the 19th and 20th centuries are easier to date from the types of fabric used. In addition, the domestic sewing machine was invented in 1845 and was in common use after 1865, so obviously a top that has been machine-pieced cannot possibly have been made any earlier than the mid-19th century.

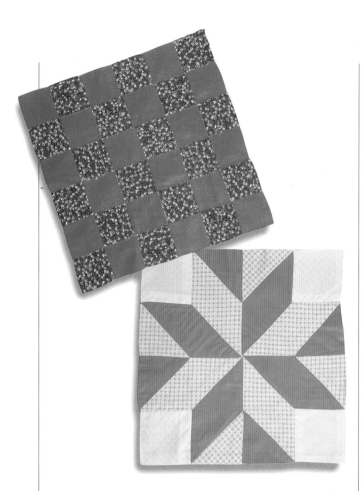

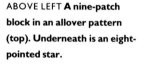

ABOVE LEFT **A nine-patch block in an allover pattern (top). Underneath is an eight-pointed star.**

ABOVE **A nine-patch block, Shoo-fly pattern (top). Underneath is a nine-patch block in a pieced and plain set.**

The construction of the top of a block patchwork quilt is referred to as a "set." There are four basic quilt sets: the edge-to-edge set; the diamond or diagonal set; the pieced and plain set; and the sashing set. These terms are largely self-explanatory.

▌The edge-to-edge set has blocks sewn directly to one another to make the whole top in a square grid.

▌The diagonal or diamond set is made from squares turned on their points.

▌The pieced and plain set is generally stitched on the square with alternate squares in plain fabric and patchwork blocks, a style that gave quilters a chance to decorate the otherwise plain blocks with intricate quilting patterns.

▌The sashing sets are those in which narrow strips of fabric are sewn between the patchwork blocks, thereby creating a frame around each square. These sashings sometimes include a small square where the strips join each other, which is known as sashing with squares. Sashing can be used with the diagonal set, but this is unusual.

ABOVE **A nine-patch block, Winged Square pattern.**

ABOVE **A nine-patch block known as eight-point design,** Variable Star, Texas Star or Lone Star.

Some block patchwork patterns themselves can look like sashing, as in the four-patch design called Churn Dash. This has a large, plain square in the center, and is pieced around the outside. When it is sewn edge-to-edge it gives a strong latticework effect. The use of more than one block can also create a lattice effect, especially when blocks are mixed with plain squares – for example, combining a variation of the Variable Star block with Sue's Choice block around the plain squares gives a lattice-type effect.

BELOW **Both these block patchwork quilts have been worked in sashing sets. The one on the left is a Churn Dash pattern in printed fabrics, with plain white pieces sewn to a pink sashing. The example on the right is a representational block of a basket, and it was** made in New Jersey in the 1920s. The block is made of plain cottons – pink for the basket and white for the ground – sewn in sashing with a square at the join. Both quilts are heavily quilted, but the quilting is more visible in the basket pattern.

SQUARES

A block of patchwork using only squares can be simple yet extremely effective. Plain and printed fabrics worked in a nine-patch block can make a cross or a chain effect, depending on where the darker or plain colored fabrics are placed in the block. If the patchwork block is pieced with many small squares and then joined with plain blocks, the effect is of a checkerboard with both large and small checks.

A simple four-patch design can be very bold. The Bow Tie pattern, for example, is four squares with a diamond in the middle, which makes an arrow or bow tie shape. When these are sewn edge-to-edge a strong diagonal stripe is created, but if they are turned so that the points meet, the center space of the four patches forms an octagon, and the overall effect is like the interlaced strips of rattan seen in canework.

ABOVE **A nine-patch pink and white block, worked on the point, has pink squares in the center and at the corners, joined in a pieced and plain set, to give the effect of a Single** **Irish Chain design on the square. The plain pink and white border has pink squares and a scalloped edge, sewn with a band of pink fabric.**

ABOVE **Nine-patch blocks of squares and plain blocks with embroidered 1920s nursery-rhyme figures. The fabric used was plain and printed, with cotton wadding, and the work has been quilted all over in a diamond pattern. These squares were very popular in the United States in the 1920s and 1930s, and they were sometimes sold in kits with the embroidery patterns prestamped on the plain block.**

RIGHT **This nine-patch block of blue and white has been worked in a pieced and plain set that looks like a Single Irish Chain. It was made in 1989.**

ABOVE **A 1991, two-block patchwork quilt has been made from one block that is a variation on an Evening Star pattern, and another that is a new block, named Sue's** **Choice. The combination of these blocks with plain squares creates an allover effect of squares with tulips on the outside edges.**

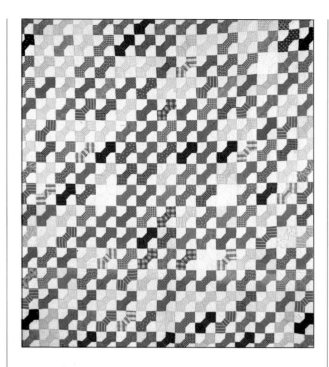

ABOVE **The Bow Tie pattern four-patch scrap quilt has been worked in an edge-to-edge set with a diamond in the center.**

This is a simple design, with a strong diagonal pattern, and it dates from the 1920s.

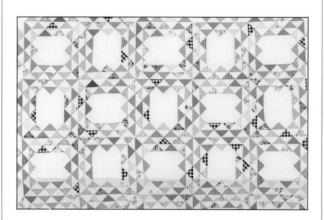

ABOVE **The Ocean Waves pattern is seen in a scrap block patchwork using triangles of scrap and white alternately in a square pattern. Because the triangles are sewn to the center square pointing in two different directions, the centers appear to be rectangles that move alternately in a vertical and a horizontal way.**

RIGHT **This example of the Flying Geese block patchwork was worked with one color for the square and triangles. The blocks are sewn edge-to-edge to give a strong diagonal design across the whole quilt, which has been pieced and quilted out to the edge.**

TRIANGLES

It is with the introduction of triangles that patchworkers really began to express themselves in their use of shapes and colors to make exciting designs. Even a quilt with only two colors can be most effective. One of these patterns, the Wild Goose Chase or Flying Geese block, creates strong diagonal lines in both directions across the top of the quilt.

Another design that uses triangles is the Lady of the Lake block, which consists of two right-angled triangles, one of which is one whole piece, while the other is a smaller, right-angled triangle with a border on the outside edges, made of even smaller, right-angled triangles. The angle and color of the small triangles in the block make them resemble a flock of geese flying over a lake or, if the colors are more spring-like, the pattern can also look like a basket.

An outstanding design can be obtained by mixing two types of patchwork block, but using only two colors. This is done by alternating a simple nine-patch block and a plain square with small colored triangles in each corner, making an octagon-shaped space in the center, known as a Melon Patch. The patterns together are known as Flagstones, Snowball, and a Four- and Nine-patch Block.

LEFT **This 1980s block patchwork uses triangles to create a strong diagonal zigzag effect. The fabric is a modern French Provençal printed cotton, originally inspired by 17th-century palampores, which is particularly obvious in the border pattern of the quilt.**

ABOVE **A sample of Castle Wall.**

LEFT **A Castle Wall block was used for this cushion cover, made in 1989. The center is an octagon formed of eight isosceles triangles.**

ABOVE **This plain red and white quilt, which dates from the 1920s, is made with two alternating blocks pieced edge-to-edge. One is a nine-patch block with a cross pattern, and the other is a four-patch block called Melon. Together they create an allover effect of canework.**

One of the earliest nine-patch blocks made was the Variable Star, which is made with squares and triangles to create an eight-pointed star shape. This pattern was used in the 18th century for corners in medallion quilts, and it was a published pattern in *Godey's Lady's Book* as early as 1862, when it was named the Godey Design. The pattern has many names – Mosaic Patchwork, Texas Star, Ohio Star, Lone Star, Flying Crow, and Happy Home – which suggests that it was well-traveled before it appeared in print. The star pattern appears in many forms, with at least a hundred patterns that have the word "star" in their names. They are frequently sewn in sashing sets or in plain and pieced sets so that the star effect is not lost.

These block patterns were beginning to be published and to become more popular at the end of the 19th century and the beginning of the 20th century. They enjoyed a strong revival in the 1920s and 1930s, but since the Great Quilt Exhibition in the 1970s they have been among the most popular of all patterns.

The number of variations of the blocks has increased in the last 20 years, and the use of color and designs has developed in new and exciting ways. The imaginative use of the simple geometric shapes is very exciting, and quilts worked in these patterns are worth collecting for the future.

BELOW **This block patchwork, called the Kaleidoscope Pinwheel, was made in Pennsylvania in the 1920s. It is** quilted all over in a diamond pattern, with a plain and printed border.

ABOVE **A star variation, nine-patch block is a simple combination of five plain squares and four squares divided into right-angled triangles. The whole squares are plain cottons, and half of each triangle is the same material as the squares, while the other half is of 1930s silk-screen-printed scraps. The quilt** is sewn together with white sashing, and it is heavily quilted in the plain blocks with a Log Cabin pattern and outline quilted inside all the triangles. The side borders and sashing are quilted with diagonal lines, and the bottom and top borders are quilted with diamond crosses.

ABOVE **This eight-pointed star patchwork is pieced edge-to-edge. It was made in the 1980s. The star is formed of diamonds, and the block is** filled out with two different types of triangle, a large light-colored isosceles triangle on the sides, and two right-angled half-squares at the corners, one light, the other dark.

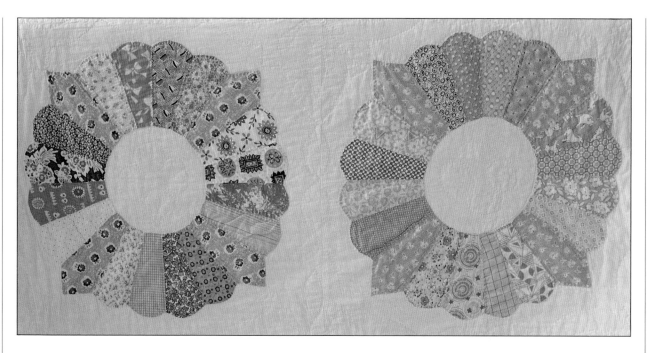

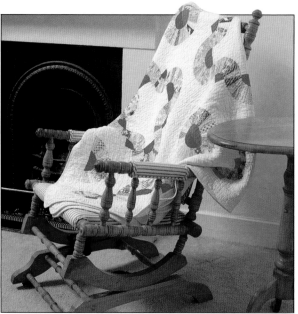

LEFT **An example of the Mohawk Trail block patchwork pattern that was made with scraps and plain red on a white ground. This is a traditional pattern, popular in New York State in the 19th century, and so called, presumably, because the Mohawk Indians were very good at leading their enemies around in circles during the French and Indian Wars. This example was made in the 1920s or 1930s, at around the same time that the Double Wedding Ring and Dresden Plate patterns were so popular.**

ABOVE **The Dresden Plate block scrap patchwork, made of 1920s and 1930s silk-screen-printed fabrics, was one of the most popular patterns in the late 19th century and early 20th century, when kits containing precut fabric patches were available. This example was not made from a kit, but is a real scrap patchwork quilt, as can be seen from the fact that the pointed pieces are not all one color, and none of the curved pieces is repeated in any of the other plates.**

CURVES AND CIRCLES

Curved and circular shapes are more difficult to stitch and to get right than the straight lines of squares and triangles. Because of this the quilts, made with these shapes were regarded as "best" quilts, and more of them have survived than the everyday ones. The names of the patterns also reveal a sense of fun – the Drunkard's Path wobbles across the quilt, and Mohawk Trail leads you around in a colorful circle.

One of the earliest circular blocks is the Dresden Plate, which was first worked in the mid-19th century, although it did not become really fashionable until the beginning of the 20th century. At this time the block was sold in kit form, with all the pieces color-matched and cut out, ready for working. This was also the case with the Double Wedding Ring block, which in fact is really more like an allover pattern than a block. Both of these patterns became extremely popular during the 1920s and 1930s.

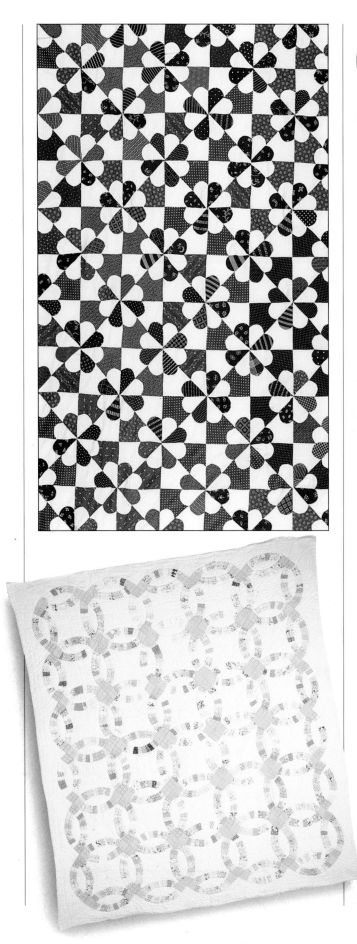

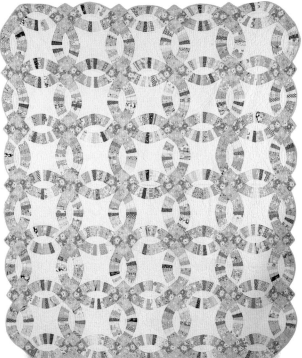

LEFT **Printed blue and plain white fabric was used in this curved design with an allover effect of mosaic tiles.**

BELOW LEFT **A scrap patchwork in the Double Wedding Ring pattern has been made with a straight border. The crosses are all the same, but the rings are placed in a more random way than in most quilts of this kind.**

ABOVE **This example of the Double Wedding Ring may have been made from a 1920s kit because the color-coordinated pieces are not as varied as in a scrap patchwork design. The borders are scalloped with a bias band on the edges.**

If a square is cut along the sides in concave shapes and then sewn onto an oval or elliptical piece, which is called a Melon shape, then the block is known as a Pin Cushion or as Robbing Peter to Pay Paul. A solid circular pattern in the center of a four-patch block is also called Robbing Peter to Pay Paul, and it looks very dramatic when it is combined with the Broken Dish pattern. When the center piece is a nine-patch block, the patchwork effect is much stronger. The Melon shape is also used in the Orange Peel, Bay Leaf, or Lover's Knot designs, as well as in the Double Wedding Ring, in which the circles overlap each other to create elegant, curved shapes.

ABOVE **This scrap patchwork of Robbing Peter to Pay Paul, which was made in the 1920s, uses a nine-patch block for the** center and has a plain white Melon shape sewn to the outside edges.

ABOVE **This Flying Squares block patchwork, made in the 1970s, uses scraps in an edge-to-edge set. Each quarter of the quilt is the same, which creates a turning square effect.**

RIGHT **Silk-screen-printed patterned fabrics from the 1920s and 1930s were used for** this block patchwork. The quilt is made of two patterns: one a Pinwheel or Broken Dish block, the other a quartered circle sewn next to a plain hourglass-shaped piece, which creates a strong diagonal effect. The plain wide border has narrow tape edges. It is heavily quilted in the patterns throughout.

REPRESENTATIONAL PATCHWORK BLOCKS

Some patchwork blocks, made up of simple geometric shapes – squares, rectangles, and triangles – actually create pictures of houses, boats, flowers, leaves, trees, or baskets. Most of the representational blocks used plain backgrounds of white or off-white to show off the designs to the best effect. The houses in the designs are believed to have originated from the old wooden schoolhouses in New Jersey, built in the middle of the 19th century. Most old examples of this pattern were made on the East Coast, and were later moved to the Midwestern states at the end of the 19th century.

Representations of baskets were being made in Baltimore and Pennsylvania at the same time. The names given to the flowers and trees tell of their origins – North Carolina Lily, Maple Leaf, Palm Leaf, and Pine Tree. It is fairly safe to assume that the boat designs originated on the East Coat as well, but there does not seem to be a record of exactly where they began. Although these are all simple shapes, they were very popular for special quilts. However, they could also be made successfully with scraps, and the basket patterns were sometimes mixed with appliquéd flowers

ABOVE **Cherry Basket blocks in a plain and patch set on the point with a random strip border. This is a good example, made in 1991, of traditional block, representational patchwork.**

BELOW **A modern (1992) representational block patchwork of a fleet of ships, made with scraps in an interpretation of a traditional design. It was inspired by the Tall Ships race, with two borders of triangles to create a wave effect.**

LEFT **This 1920s representational patchwork contains a block of houses. Two of the houses are different, either accidentally or because the maker deliberately avoided perfection in order not to offend God.**

BELOW **This representational boat or Tall Ships block, which uses bright primary and secondary colors on a white ground, has been sewn edge-to-edge to make a crib-sized quilt. It has wide and narrow borders, and was made in 1989.**

and fruits, while the handles on some were also appliquéd on. The baskets were a popular element of the Friendship Quilts, in which each basket would have been made by a different person and friend. Some of these are signed and dated pieces.

Early quilts were usually made from scraps, and are very brightly colored. The ones produced after the 1950s have tended to use pastel shades, and are not as bold. More modern examples of representational blocks have been made for children's beds and wall hangings, with boats being a particular favorite for boys' rooms, and baskets and flowers for girls' rooms.

LOOKING AFTER YOUR QUILTS

CHAPTER 8

If you are going to collect quilts, there are a few guidelines to the care of any textile that you must remember. The three worst enemies of fabrics are light, dust, and water. If you are going to use the quilts, make sure that they are in good condition to start with.

The best place for a quilt is on a bed – after all, this was the reason it was made – but, if you have more quilts than beds and, like so many collectors, simply like to see them around, they can be used in a variety of ways. The only proviso is that when they are draped or displayed they should never be in direct sunlight. Fabrics fade very quickly in strong light, which can also weaken the cloth at the same time. If a quilt is over the back of a chair or sofa, it should be away from a window. Artificial light, especially fluorescent lights, can also fade fabrics. Strong spotlights trained on a quilt that is hanging against a wall will damage it with heat, and will also attract dust. Dry dust will penetrate the weave of the cloth and block up the holes that give fabrics their softness and flexibility, so, if building work, plastering, or redecorating is going to be done in your home, all your quilts should be sealed away until the work is completed.

Water can stain a quilt, and once a fabric is stained there is no way of removing the mark. Old quilts sometimes have brown marks on them that look like rust; this, too, is unremovable. However, if you can live with a few spots, the history of the quilt itself will come alive for you.

Quilts that are going to be used every day will wear out faster than those used for a few months each year, so if possible, it is a good idea to circulate your quilts every three or four months. Changing them with the seasons is a good system, and they will all last longer.

ABOVE LEFT **In an ideal world, all quilt-makers, collectors, and enthusiasts would have a piece of furniture like this. It is the top of a dresser with large, sliding drawers, originally made for shirts. When you store quilts, you should keep them folded as loosely as possible, with as few folds as are necessary to get them into the storage space. You should also avoid stacking them up more than three or four deep, otherwise the bottom one will be crushed. Line the cupboard, box, or trunk in which they are stored with acid-free paper.**

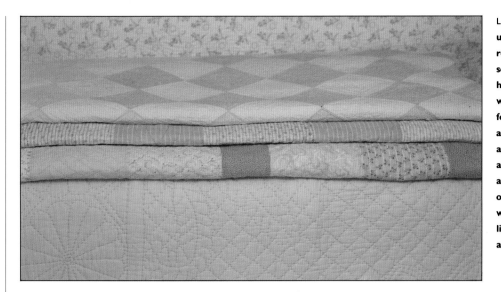

LEFT **If you are collecting and using quilts, it is a good idea to rotate them through the seasons. The bottom quilt is a heavy wholecloth quilt with wool padding, which is suitable for winter. The next three are allover patchwork quilts with a variety of padding weights and color shades that are appropriate for different times of year. The one at the top is a wholecloth quilt that is very lightweight in both padding and color.**

CLEANING

When you buy a quilt, ask the seller if it has been treated in any way. If the answer is "yes," ask how the quilt has been cleaned, because it is not advisable to mix different dry cleaning fluids with each other, or with detergents or soaps.

If the surface of the quilt needs cleaning, the best way to do it is with a vacuum cleaner, through a mesh screen of fine, stiff needlework canvas that has been tacked or stapled onto a wooden frame or canvas stretchers. This will make the canvas easy to pick up and put down as well as prevent the quilt being sucked into the vacuum. Lay the quilt out on a large, flat surface, such as a bed or a sheet on the floor, place the frame down on the quilt with the canvas directly next to it, fit the upholstery nozzle to the vacuum cleaner set to its lowest setting, and move it across the quilt. This should be done slowly and gently, and remember that you should never rest the nozzle directly on the mesh or on the quilt.

WASHING

If the quilt is made of cotton and there are no obvious holes, it may be possible to wash it. First, however, you must test the colors for fastness. This is done by placing a damp piece of white blotting paper on each colored piece and patting it gently. If any color comes out, do not wash the quilt, although it may be dry cleaned if really necessary. Also, if the fabrics are glazed, like the pre-1980s chintzes, they need to be dry cleaned or you will lose the glazing. After the 1980s, some cottons were glazed with a plastic coating, and these should be washed and not dry cleaned. If you are buying a quilt from the maker, make sure that you get the cleaning instructions. Also ask if the fabrics have been pre-shrunk, in case you want to wash the quilt in the future.

If you are going to wash a quilt, you must consider what material was used as padding. If the padding is cotton wadding and quilting is minimal, or if the padding is wool, the quilt should be hand washed. If there is a lot of quilting – covering most of the quilt and not leaving any spaces larger than 6 square inches unquilted – and the fabric is whole as well as color-fast, there is no reason why the quilt cannot go into the washing machine. It should be washed on a wool setting with a mild detergent. If the quilt does not fit in your domestic machine with a lot of space around it, take it to a laundrette. Quilts like this may be tumble dried on a cool setting, but they must not be tumble dried if the padding is wool or a synthetic fiber. It is much safer just to lay the damp quilt out flat on a large cotton sheet with towels or newspaper underneath, in a shady place outdoors or a warm, dry place inside to let it dry naturally.

If the quilt is made of silk, satin, chintz, wool, or a mixture of any of these, it should not be washed or – unless absolutely necessary – even dry cleaned. If there are holes in the quilt, embroidery stitches, or beads – or if you have any doubts at all – take the quilt to an expert in cleaning delicate materials, like wedding dresses, or ask a museum for advice. Sometimes the best thing to do when in doubt is nothing.

HAND WASHING If the quilt is to be hand washed, it can be done in a bathtub or in an inflatable child's swimming pool outdoors in the shade on a warm, dry day. First, fold the quilt loosely, accordion-style. The water should be only just warm, and the detergent must be mild. Fill the tub or pool with enough water to cover the quilt, add the detergent, and make sure it is completely dissolved in the water. Then gently place the quilt in the water and press it down using the flat of your hands, so that all the quilt gets wet. It may take as long as 10–15 minutes for all the air to be released from between the layers of the quilt. Once the quilt is wet, leave it to soak for at least one hour. You may move it around a little in the water, but you must never try to lift it out while it is holding all that water.

Drain out the washing water and add fresh water to rinse. Continue to do this three or four times, making sure that the last rinse is clear. Drain the water for the final time and leave the quilt to drain for 10 minutes. When no more water runs out of the quilt, it may be removed from the bath. Because it will still be heavy and very wet, it is a good idea not to lift it by yourself, but with another pair of hands. Also, because of the weight and possible stress on the fabrics, it is advisable to slip a plastic sheet under the quilt before starting to lift it. This can be done by rolling the quilt to one side of the bath and putting half of the plastic up against it, with the other half flat in front of you. Then roll the quilt back towards you, pulling the second half of the plastic out, and returning the quilt to the way it was originally. This will help to support the wet quilt, and prevent the rest of the house from getting wet when the quilt is moved to where it is going to be dried.

To move the quilt without causing any prolonged or unnecessary strain on the fabrics and stitching, place a large tray or piece of board across one end of the bath, and then, when you lift up the wet quilt, put it directly onto the board with the plastic sheet, fold the plastic over the quilt, and lift the board.

DRYING If possible, dry the quilt outdoors in a shady, grassy spot. Prepare a drying place using several layers of thick towels, or a combination of newspapers and towels, under a large cotton sheet that is a bit larger than the quilt. Before moving the wet quilt to the drying spot, place several other thick towels under and on top of it and press out some of the excess water. Then, ideally with the help of another person, unfold the quilt gently and lay it out flat on the drying area, right side up, and allow it to dry thoroughly. Do not expose it to direct light or heat.

If you do not have space outside or if the weather is unsuitable, the drying can be done indoors. It is a good idea to put plastic sheeting down before the newspaper, towels, and sheet to prevent the carpet or flooring from getting wet. When the quilt is dry, lift it from the sheet to get some air underneath to make sure it dries completely. It is all right to lift it at this stage because it will no longer be heavy with water.

STORAGE

To store a quilt it may be folded and laid flat in a cool, dark, and dry place. The best way to fold a quilt is not just down the center, because this will eventually make a permanent crease that will fade and wear out. A quilt should be folded with the right side out. First fold the two sides into the center, and then fold these sides in again to the center. This will pad the center fold, and any creases will be on the lining.

Another way to fold it is in thirds, and not along the center at all. Whichever way it is folded, the long strip is then folded like an accordion into a square or rectangle, so that there is no great build-up of fabric along any fold that will squeeze or pull the fabric. How

ABOVE **When you fold quilts for storage, turn the large creases so that they are not all** **on one side and therefore do not crush one another.**

many folds are needed will, of course, depend where the quilt will be stored, but the fewer folds the better. Acid-free tissue paper, pleated into the folds, will help to prevent the fabric being crushed.

It is now possible to buy special racks to store quilts when they are not being used. These look very attractive, but they, too, must be kept out of direct sunlight for the sake of the quilts.

If you have several quilts to store, do not stack them in piles of more than about three. More than this, and the weight on the bottom one will crush the creases hard into it. It is also a good idea to turn the quilts so that the folds are not all on the same side.

Even if they are stored in ideal conditions, you should take out your quilts at least once a year, spread them out, refold them along different lines, and then replace them. They will look nicer and last longer for the airing. It is also an excuse to change things around and to enjoy the fine work on the quilts.

REPAIR

If you are an experienced needleworker, it is possible to repair an old quilt, but if you do, it is best to try to match the original fabrics with something that is approximately the same age and color. You should also

make a record of the repair with "before" and "after" photographs to go with the quilt as part of its history.

Never take anything out of patchwork or appliqué; patch over the original worn pieces, attaching the new pieces with invisible slipstitches or ladder stitches to the healthy and strong fabric around the hole. It is almost impossible to repair the fabric of wholecloth quilted quilts without the new work being obvious. Sometimes it is best not to try to repair it. Simply do enough to ensure that the wadding does not come out and the hole gets no worse. This can be done by slipping a fine, transparent fabric over the hole, and stitching around the hole with tiny stitches.

RELINING

If heavy covers – the Victorian Hexagons and Tumbling Blocks, for example – have not been quilted, they often need relining, because the weight of the top means that the lining takes a lot of wear and tear. If you want to give these pieces a new life, it is sometimes a good idea to take off the back and put the top onto a sheet of clean cotton or flannel. Tack the pieced top to this interlining, as you would the interlinings of curtains, with long stitches. Then reattach the original lining or a replacement, if it is needed, stitching this in the same manner as the top, but going across instead of up and down. The fabric in the middle will now take the weight and support the top as well as the back.

REPAIR OF A DOUBLE WEDDING RING QUILT

This set of pictures shows the repair of a section of a Double Wedding Ring Quilt. Each of the small sections shown below illustrates a different stage in the repair process. You need to exercise great care at all times when handling old and delicate fabrics, because they are likely to tear easily.

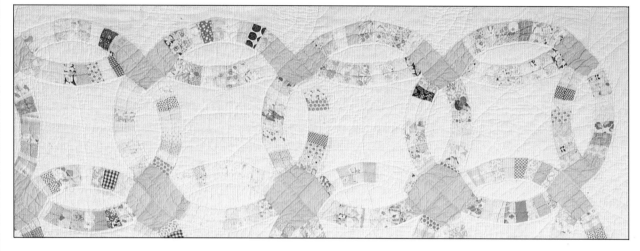

ABOVE **The section of the quilt that is to be repaired where the old material is tearing and disintegrating in several places.**

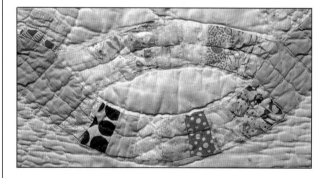

ABOVE **This was the condition of one of the sections of the quilt before repair. You can see where the padding is showing through the torn fabric.**

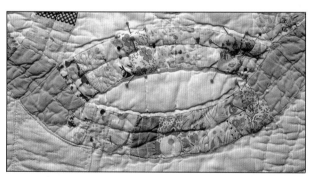

ABOVE **Here the new pieces are pinned firmly in place, with the edges turned in, ready for sewing. The new pieces will be stitched down with a ladder stitch.**

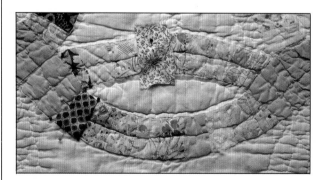

ABOVE **On this section, a new piece of material is pinned over the worn and disintegrating fabric. It has been carefully selected to match the original material.**

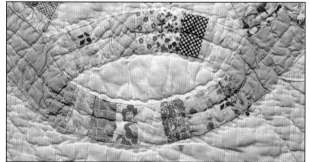

ABOVE **This shows the completed repairs. The pieces with pins are the new pieces. You can see where the new quilting has been completed through these.**

GLOSSARY

Appliqué work – creating a design by placing or applying one fabric onto a background fabric and sewing it onto the ground cloth with small holding stitches.

Broderie perse – French for Persian Embroidery; a type of appliqué work. Fabrics are stiffened with glue and paper on the wrong side, and then cut out in shapes and stitched onto a background, with a cord couched around the cut or raw edges. Now it also means cutting out a printed design to be appliquéd.

Chintz – a Hindi word meaning spotted or printed cloth. Originally chintz was block-printed and/or handpainted cotton fabric from India. Today we think of chintz as a plain or printed cotton fabric that is glazed.

Indiennes cloth – the French name for printed cotton imported from India.

Linsey-woolsey – a linen and wool fabric with a warp made of linen and a weft made of wool that was not good enough to be spun into a long, strong thread suitable for a warp.

Palampore – the Hindi and Persian word for a printed and/or handpainted cotton bedspread. The originals were printed on a dark red ground in the style of Persian carpets. Later, they were printed on a plain bleached or unbleached background, with the Tree of Life and flower designs in the center, surrounded by borders.

Pintado – the Portuguese name for printed cotton fabrics imported from India.

Quilt – a cover or coverlet made by stitching one cloth over another, generally with some soft padding between the layers. The top cloth can be wholecloth, patchwork pieced, or appliquéd.

Quilting – the stitching holding the layers of a quilt together.

Trapunto – stuffed and/or padded quilting, also known as bas-relief quilting. It originated in the 14th century in Sicily.

Whitework – embroidery on white material with white threads which was used for bed linen, tablecloths, cushions, curtains, and lingerie. It includes cutwork, pulled thread, eyelet holes, and decorative edges.

Wholecloth quilts – quilts whose top and back are made of lengths of the same material (cotton, linen, or wool, etc.).

BIBLIOGRAPHY

BATH, V. CHURCHILL. *Needlework in America*, Mills & Boon Ltd., 1979

BEYER, J. *The Art and Technique of Creating Medallion Quilts*, E.P.M. Publications Inc., 1982

BEYER, J. *The Quilters' Album of Blocks and Borders*, E.P.M. Publications Inc., 1980; Bell & Hyman Ltd., 1982

CLABBURN, P. *Masterpieces of Embroidery*, Phaidon Press Ltd., 1981

COLBY, A. *Patchwork Quilts*, B. T. Batsford Ltd., 1965

COLBY, A. *Quilting*, B. T. Batsford Ltd., 1972

FITZRANDOLPH, M. AND FLETCHER, F. M. *Quilting*, The Dryad Press, 1972

ICKIS, M. *The Standard Book of Quilt Making and Collecting*, Dover Publications Inc., 1949

MONTGOMERY, F. M. *Textiles in America, 1650–1870*, W. W. Norton & Co., A Winterthur/Barra Book, 1984

ORLOFSKY, P. AND M. *Quilts in America*, McGraw-Hill Book Co., 1974; Abbeville Press Publishers, (Reprint) 1992

PAINE, M. *Textile Classics*, Mitchell Beazley International Ltd., 1990

PELLMAN, R. AND K. *A Treasury of Amish Quilts*, Good Books, 1990

SEWARD, L. *The Complete Book of Patchwork, Quilting, and Appliqué*, Mitchell Beazley, 1987

SEWARD, L. *Country Quilts*, Mitchell Beazley International Ltd., 1987

STOREY, J. *Textile Printing*, Thames & Hudson, 1974

WENTWORTH, J. "English Patchwork Covers," *Antique Collecting*, Vol. 23, No. 4, 1988

WILSON, E. *Quilts of America*, Oxmoor House Inc., 1979

WISS, A. AND W. *Folk Quilts and How To Recreate Them*, The Main Street Press, 1983

USEFUL ADDRESSES AND MUSEUMS

USEFUL ADDRESSES

U.S.A.

American Folk Gallery (Steven
Miller), 17 East 96th Street,
New York, New York 10028

American Hurrah Antiques, 766
Madison Avenue, New York,
New York 10021

M. Finkel & Daughter, 936 Pine Street,
Philadelphia, Pennsylvania 19107

Great Expectations Quilts Inc., 14520
Memorial, Suite 54, Houston, Texas
77079

Quilts of America, Elaine Sloan Hart,
431 East 73rd Street, New York, New
York 10021

U.K.

Judy Greenwood Antiques, 657 Fulham
Road, London SW6 5PY

Jo Peters, Foxhill Agencies,
"Ropemakers," River, Petworth,
West Sussex GU28 9AY

The Quilt Room, 20 West Street,
Dorking, Surrey RH4 1BL

Ron Simpson, London,
By appointment, tel: 071-727 0983

Judy Wentworth, The Textile Company,
P.O. Box 2800, London N1 4DO

MUSEUMS

CANADA

Royal Ontario Museum,
Toronto, Ontario

DENMARK

Danish Folk Museum, Copenhagen

Kunstindustrimuseet/Museum of
Decorative Arts, Bredgade 68,
Copenhagen

FINLAND

Finnish National Museum, Helsinki

FRANCE

Musée des Arts Decoratifs, 107 Rue de
Rivoli, Paris

Musée des Arts et Traditions
Populaires, Bois de Boulogne, Paris

GERMANY

Altonaer Museum, Hamburg

Deutsche Volkskrunde, Berlin

GREECE

Benaki Museum, Athens

Museum of Greek Folk Art, Athens

HOLLAND

Arnhem Open Air Museum, Arnhem

Willet-Holthuysen Museum,
Amsterdam

ITALY

Il Museo Stibbert, Villa Montughi,
Florence

NORWAY

Norwegian Folk Museum, Oslo

SPAIN

Museo Lazaro Galdiano, Madrid

Museo Nacional de Artes Decoratiras,
Montalbán 12, Madrid

SWEDEN

Nordic Folk Museum, Stockholm

Goteborgs Koustmuseum, Gotaplatsen,
Goteborg (Gothenburg)

SWITZERLAND

Schwizerisches Landesmuseum, Zurich

U.S.A.

Baltimore Museum of Art, Art Museum
Drive, Baltimore, Maryland 21218

Cincinnati Art Museum, Eden Park,
Cincinnati, Ohio 45202

The Henry Francis du Pont Winterthur
Museum, Winterthur, Delaware
19735

Museum of American Folk Art, 49 West
53rd Street, New York, New York
10019

Shelburne Museum, U.S. Route 7,
Shelburne, Vermont 05482

U.K.

Royal Scottish Museum, Edinburgh,
Scotland

Victoria and Albert Museum, Cromwell
Road, London SW7

Worthing Museum and Art Gallery,
Chapel Road, Worthing, West Sussex
BN11 1HP

INDEX

Italic page numbers refer to picture captions.

ACKNOWLEDGEMENTS

t = top, b = bottom, m = middle, l = left, r = right

The author and publisher wish to thank the following people and organizations for lending their quilts to be photographed. Other quilts pictured in the book belong to private collections.

PHILIPPA ABRAHAMS: page 71b.
MARGARET ARMSTRONG: page 62br.
MARY ANN CORP: pages 37t; 42; 70b.
FRANCES DEXTER: pages 53b; 59t.
JACKIE HITCHEN: page 24b.

IKUKO OBATO: pages 54tl; 70t.
JO PETERS: pages 19b; 26m; 27t; 64b; 66t & bl.
THE QUILT ROOM: pages 16t; 17t; 19t; 34; 41b; 45b; 58b; 62t; 64t & m; 65mr; 66br; 68tl & r; 69t; 71t.
SHEILA ROMAIN: page 47t.
RON SIMPSON: pages 19m; 25; 31t & b; 43t; 45t.

SUE SUMPTER: page 63.
WORTHING MUSEUM AND ART GALLERY: pages 6; 9t & b; 18tl, tr, bl & br; 21b; 32t & b; 33t; 36; 37b; 39; 40t; 41t; 43br; 49t; 50t & b; 51b; 52b; 53t; 54tr & br.